THE KING OF
HIGHBANKS ROAD

THE
KING OF
HIGHBANKS
ROAD

Rediscovering Dad, Rural America, and
Learning to Love Home Again

STEVE WATKINS
FOREWORD BY JAMES L. RUBART

THE KING OF HIGHBANKS ROAD
Rediscovering Dad, Rural America,
and Learning to Love Home Again

720 Odell Trail
Jonesboro, AR 72401

STEVE@STEVE-WATKINS.COM

Copyright © 2020 Pilgrim Publishing

ISBN: 978-1-7356952-1-1

Table of Contents

FOREWORD by James L. Rubart viii

INTRODUCTION.................................... 1

Chapter 1: A Second Chance............................ 7

Chapter 2: Gut Gravity................................ 12

Chapter 3: Numbing.................................. 15

Chapter 4: The King is Crowned 21

Chapter 5: Duck Woods................................ 24

Chapter 6: Deafening Silence 32

Chapter 7: A Land That Lived 38

Chapter 8: His Kingdom 45

Chapter 9: Constant Craving 52

Chapter 10: Strongholds: The Farm & the Father Wound ... 55

Chapter 11: Just Enough Jesus to be Miserable.............. 63

Chapter 12: Barber Shops 76

Chapter 13: Fence Rows............................... 80

Chapter 14: The Art of Loafing in a Parts Store............. 86

Chapter 15: The Wrecking Ball & a Rite of Passage 91

Chapter 16: Lord, Bring a Hurricane 97

Chapter 17: Country Folk.............................. 105

Chapter 18: Fish Fries & BBQs 115

Chapter 19: Trot Lines & 'Talphy Worms 121

Chapter 20: Let Them Eat Corn 129

Chapter 21: Purple Birds & The Performance Gospel 135

Chapter 22: The Hog Lady 143

Chapter 23: Jail Talk 146

Chapter 24: The Last Lie 152

Chapter 25: Judge Not 156

Chapter 26: Her Majesty 165

Chapter 27: Prince of Shame: An Unwinnable Paradox 170

Chapter 28: Biscuits & Gravy 173

Chapter 29: Nothing to Forgive 178

Chapter 30: The Reckless Pursuit of Grace 182

Chapter 31: Perfect Peace: Behold the Proof 191

Chapter 32: Fathers, Sons & The Father 196

AFTERWORD 200

FOREWORD BY JAMES L. RUBART

Fair warning—after you finish *The King of Highbanks Road*, you'll want Steve Watkins to be your new best friend.

I'm not kidding.

You'll become so ensconced in the world Steve paints and the person Steve is, that you'll dream of spending an afternoon sitting next to him in a chair that rocks without a sound, looking out over a river where the catfish are plentiful and the smell of barbecue fills the air.

Here's the good news: I guarantee you (and I haven't asked Steve this, but I'm still guaranteeing it) if you were to email Steve and say, "I'm coming by to meet you to talk about simple pleasures and complex ponderings and everything in-between," he'd email back telling you to hurry, that there's a cold one waiting for you with plenty of stories still to be told.

And here's the kicker. He'd absolutely 100 percent mean it.

Yes, he's that kind of real. He's a man with that kind of heart.

Steve and I met in 2015, but we became true friends at a writing retreat in the fall of 2019. Kind of impossible not to like the guy. Well, actually, fall in love with him. If he's your friend, he'll go to the wall for you and give of himself with absolutely no expectation of return. That's exactly what he did for my wife as he helped her explore a solo adventure trip overseas, acting as if she were his long-lost sister.

So when Steve asked me to write the foreword to his book my answer was immediate. "Yes!" (And that was before I read it.) Why? Because I knew the book would stir emotions deep inside me; take me away to a world I've heard about but have never truly understood; give me penetrating insight into a friend that has become a brother.

If you're like me, you'll get misty in the eyes a few times, and you'll also bask in the stories, the people, the vividly painted scenes and truths of life in 1980s Arkansas. I think immersed is the right word for what you're about to experience. Yep, I'm going with immersed ... in wisdom and vulnerability and deep insight into the human condition.

Especially between fathers and sons.

Maybe that's why Steve asked me. Because I get it, just like he does. How fragile the relationship between a father and a son can be. How sticks and stones bruise for a moment, but words spoken (or not spoken) can slice you open every day for the rest of your life. But also that restoration is possible even when there looks to be no hope, and the truth that God is the great healer of broken hearts.

This is a book for dads and sons, yes. But it's also for the moms, the sisters, the friends who are such an integral part of their lives.

One more quick thought and then I'll let you get to it.

Steve is a talented writer. He writes raw and real, polished and gritty, unfiltered and nuanced, with phrases that settle on you like a dandelion spore, as well as ones that splash down like a five-gallon bucket of water on a cooker of a summer day.

In other words, you're in for a serious treat.

(And don't forget to tell Steve hi for me when you drop by),

James L. Rubart
New York Times Best-Selling Author
September 2020

ACKNOWLEDGEMENTS

Producing a self-published book that meets or exceeds the standards of most traditionally published books takes time, planning, learning from lots of past mistakes, coordination, and a superb team. It's not unlike conducting an orchestra - just with hundreds of emails, texts, and video chats.

The extraordinary team that helped create my first book, *Pilgrim Strong*, reunited (with a few additions) to produce *The King of Highbanks Road*. It's true what a wise mentor shared nearly two decades ago: No one ever achieves anything significant without someone else's help.

James L. Rubart is one of my favorite people in the world. He's a man who uses his God-given gifts to help others experience a greater freedom in life through his amazing storytelling. But Jim, a New York Times best-selling author, is more than a great storyteller. He's plain and simple, just a good man, and that's what I love about him most. It's one of my life's great honors that he'd pen the foreword for this book and set the tone for helping readers understand what it's truly about from chapter one onward.

My sincere thanks and respect to developmental editor Beth Jusino, who is also my friend, fellow pilgrim, and tattoo twin.

Beth and I were friends before our professional relationship, and we questioned whether crossing that boundary was a good idea. It surely was. We're a solid team.

Line editor Amy Horton came aboard this time and cleaned up the messes I'd read across so often they could no longer be detected. She is also the project director for our companion cookbook. Amy is the kind of person you want in your corner when things need getting done. Having someone you trust handling things that are so important to you is an invaluable blessing.

Keith Richardson, a man for whom I have respect on so many levels, hit cleanup with a final edit just days before publication that gave me a closing peace to this book. Keith is another man worth anyone's aspirations.

Colleen Sheehan has now designed four covers and two book interiors across five years of my career. She bears with my every visual whim, good or bad, and always works magic in the end creating a face to the story that I usually think about every day for two years. Her job is so important, and I love what she's done, in particular, with this cover. It captures the very essense of my father doing what he loved, in control, in the moment.

Hanne Pelletier is the graphic artist responsible for the pencil sketch visuals. If we were going to pull off something visual in this book, it had to be oh, so perfect, and feel just right. Thanks for going down this road with me once again, Hanne.

Something special happened somewhere along my 2015 pilgrimage across Spain as I shared that quest on social media and in real time. I formed a tribe that just keeps growing. Several thousand people came along for that experience, cheering, adding substantive thoughts, and offering encouragement along the Way. You've been with me ever since, and to call you family is no exaggeration. I love you guys, and have such gratitude that you're in

my life because you've played such an important part of changing my life for the good.

Finally, to my family, especially my wife, Dana, and my mom,
who have endured all the moodiness, all the emotions, and all the
disquietude brought about when you revisit memories like this
for two years, thanks is not enough. I love you both, and don't
know that any of this would have gotten done were it not for your
encouragement.

The best thing you can ever tell someone is how much you
believe in them. Thank you both for believing.

DEDICATION

Dedicated to all those who ever lived and loved in rural America. To those who drank from a well with a rusty pump handle, those who formed callouses from the end of a hoe, ate watermelon right out of the field, and to those who did the back-breaking work of pulling a pick sack through the cool, morning dew of fall.

But dedicated most of all to my amazing mother, the Queen of Highbanks Road. For without the queen, there would have been no king, and I might never have witnessed the strength and unconditional love that can manifest through every circumstance. Thank you for the freedom to tell this story just as it needed telling. But mostly, thank you for being a wonderful mom to that farm boy, and a best friend to the man who evolved from all those experiences we shared. I love you forever.

All that I am, or hope to be,
I owe to my angel mother.

-Abraham Lincoln

THE KING'S ENGLISH

Some favorite phrases David Watkins frequently used.

- She's as nervous as a sinner in church. (as nervous as it gets)
- Never get in a fight with a pig in the mud. You get dirty, and the pig loves it. (some things just aren't worth it)
- He's choppin' in tall cotton. (acknowledging a nice accomplishment)
- Don't know about you, but I'm wore plum out. (more than just tired — very tired)
- How's your mom and them? (greeting between families close in friendship)
- You beat all I've ever seen. (hard to believe)
- Colder than a well digger's @$#. (very cold)
- He's gettin' way too big for his britches. (braggart)
- Slow as molasses in winter. (usually reserved to describe an adolescent male)
- I'm full as a tick. (what you say after every meal in the South)
- Look to the West. It's comin' up a storm. (rain and wind will be here in twenty minutes)
- I'll swan. (my, oh, my)
- Yes, sir, that (rain) was a toad strangler. (rain that leaves water standing in row middles)
- Tight as a banjo string. (a cheap old man, or a nut on a bolt that won't budge)
- I swear to my time. (personal exasperation, disbelief)
- He doesn't know his @$# from a hole in the ground. (downright dumb)
- He's cruisin' for a bruisin'. (luck is about to run out)
- Picked it clean. (reference to the garden - leaving nothing behind)

THE KING OF
HIGHBANKS ROAD

INTRODUCTION

There are those who will swim to the shore, and those who will cling to the broken pieces.

unknown

At some point this side of eternity, everyone searches for themselves. Some meaning. Some purpose. Some deeper understanding of who they are, and why they are that way. Generally, we complicate this uncomplicated quest. Look much further past your mom or your dad, or the culture where you grew up, and you've probably gone too far. Blessing or curse, we are authentic products of the place and circumstances from which we come.

I avoided the search for forty years until there was no other choice but to run toward it intentionally, and like a wild man who's come to a place where the consequences are inconsequential, and the self-discoveries be damned.

Somewhere along the way in my formative years, someone called it the U.S. Farm Crisis, and the label stuck. One psychologist who counseled widow after grieving widow called it a wrecking ball that blindsided rural America. Another academic described it simply as "ungodly hell."

I called it childhood.

Time and random circumstance will connect you to something so strongly that you become oblivious to the warning signs. That's what happened to me, though I was just a kid who wanted nothing more than to fit into the small-town group of popular kids and misfits who were my peers.

Sometimes when you're living through something big (like some era that will eventually, but does not yet have a name), you just keep living through it because that's all you know. That place, that circumstance, that moment in time is normal because you know nothing else. It's *your* normal.

But the reality is that deep inside there's a context somewhere outside your understanding. Truth is, you may be living in the prime of something grand, or the bowels of a monster. But you keep living, keep smiling, keep doing your best, no matter the twinge in your belly, or even when you cry yourself to sleep three nights running.

I never knew what to call it, but my childhood and adolescent *normal* always felt odd — something strange and out of the ordinary. There were happy occasions, but we never knew much peace.

And there is nothing normal or peaceful about the expectation that every new day would be the one when the phone would ring and someone on the other end would explain how they'd found my father in a ditch with his head blown off by a .12 gauge shotgun. That was my normal for the longest, until I compartmentalized it from memory through most of adult life.

It was long after I'd decided to write this book, near the manuscript's final edits and while doing some research, that I discovered a recent article from *The Guardian* titled: *Why Are America's Farmers Killing Themselves?* A few days later, a colleague sent this clipping from *USA Today*: *Midwestern Farmers Face a Crisis: Hundreds Are Dying By Suicide.*

As it turns out, this story of father and son and place and time traces its roots to that ungodly childhood Hell of the 1980s. It is since that time that farmers are now among the most likely of all professions to take their own lives.

As I read these stories of middle-aged men — some veterans, others school board members, all fathers and husbands — who'd become so saddled with debt, overwhelmed with change, and guilt-ridden by the prospect of losing their land and failing a family legacy, the tears wouldn't stop streaming. I'd blocked these memories for thirty-five years thinking there would never be cause to revisit them.

That I had the chance to do that very thing may be one of the best parts of my life story, and an ongoing healing that not everyone gets.

As it turns out, rural America finds itself in the midst of a new crisis today, the threat perhaps even greater than the 1980s wrecking ball:

- Farm bankruptcy rates are at an all-time high.
- Extreme weather and falling prices have bludgeoned dairy and crop producers in recent years, so much so that nearly twenty million acres were not planted during the 2019 farm season.
- Trade tensions have reduced exports as much as seventy-five percent.
- Farmer suicides have jumped more than forty percent during the last two decades.

It is, in fact, a global crisis. An Australian farmer dies by suicide every four days. In the UK, one farmer a week takes his or her own life. In France, one farmer dies by suicide every two days. In India, more than 270,000 farmers have died by suicide since 1995. Every thirty minutes an Indian farmer ends his own life.

Dr. Michael Rosman's name stood out in the articles and among the research. Rosman was passionate enough about the plight he saw in his home state of Iowa that he left seminary to become a clinical psychologist, and one of America's leading experts on rural American behavioral science. He's counseled hundreds of families who endured traumatic loss.

In 1999, Rosman joined an effort called Sowing Seeds of Hope, and connected uninsured and underinsured farmers in seven midwestern states to affordable behavioral health services. In 2001, he became its executive director. For the next fourteen years, the organization fielded approximately a half-million telephone calls from farmers, trained over 10,000 rural behavioral health professionals, and provided subsidized behavioral health resources to more than 100,000 farm families.

Reading at the kitchen table, I was overwhelmed both with the enormity of the problem, and Michael Rosman's heart.

My Lord, I wasn't just imagining all this. We really were living through something extraordinary, and just didn't know it. Our normal was a God-awful Hell. And it's happening again!

Now, armed with key phrases like "farmer suicide" and "behavioral health in rural America," I found research articles by the dozens. I didn't know whether to laugh and celebrate, or to keep crying.

In another five minutes I'd done enough research to uncover Dr. Rosman's contact information, and sent him a quick email:

Dr. Rosman: I'm a child of the 1980s raised on a small cotton farm in Arkansas. I knew we were living through something extraordinary back then, I just didn't know what. I lived every day, believing it would be my father's last, and so many things about life on the farm have, for better or worse, shaped who I am today. In fact, I'm in the final chapters of writing a book about it all. I'm thrilled to find out this is a cause to which you've dedicated your life and wonder if you might be willing to speak with me.

Not knowing whether I'd ever hear from him, I hit *send*, then buried my head in my hands to cry some more. Suddenly everything felt raw again. But the story I'd written during the last eighteen months felt more real now, and it had a distinctive purpose. Maybe sharing this story would actually help some people in my generation better understand themselves.

My phone rang the next afternoon.

"Steve, this is Mike Rosman. I got your message this morning. I'm retired now, and I actually don't talk to many people about this anymore, but I could feel the passion in your email, and I wanted to give you a call back. What can I do for you?" he asked.

For the next ten minutes we spoke about family, religion, weather, politics in agriculture, the eighties, fathers, and legacies in the land, as if we'd known each other a lifetime. For the first time it was as if someone understood me at a soul level — a place I'd pushed from memory long ago. It was like the rebirth of something long dead. I apologized for my profuse crying.

"You go ahead and cry about it, son. I know exactly how you feel. You just let it out."

That was the moment that changed everything about this book.

This is not just a story about me and my farm-family raising. It's a story about a culture and a set of circumstances that spiraled out of control and touched human lives in the deepest and most long-lasting ways. An entire generation is the way it is today because it survived the wrecking ball. If for no other reason, the story needs telling for those who didn't.

Because somewhere out there in rural Nebraska, or Iowa, or Alabama, a 10-year-old farm kid is curled up in a ball right now, living it all over again.

CHAPTER 1

A Second Chance

Being deeply loved by someone gives you strength, while loving someone deeply gives you courage.

Lao Tzu

It was a feeling I'd felt only a couple of times before. The one where a voice from some distant place speaks to you so clearly what needs to be done, and how you are the one to do it. And how the time is not some distant future date, but rather this very moment. It was in that moment instinct came alive.

Do this now. It completely permeated my being.

And I knew the voice's source, which made fighting it a struggle all too pointless. If anything, that knowledge intensified my churning gut.

God was so clearly telling me to do something so radically and uncomfortably different than anything I'd done for my father over the last twenty years that as I stalled for time driving back and forth along the street where he lived, I barely threw the truck door open in time to vomit toward the sewer main. I'll never believe the policeman who stopped alongside completely bought the explanation about nerves, and that I was about to have a very difficult conversation with my sixty-five-year-old dad. But I'd never been more stone-cold sober, and he gave me a wary pass.

Two hours earlier in the morning rush of getting three children ready for school and daycare, and already consumed mentally with a work checklist a mile long, I'd completely forgotten the day's significance. Herding three kids toward the Tahoe and on to their morning drop-offs, I nearly closed the door behind me when my wife prompted the reminder.

"You know it's your dad's birthday," she said.

I dropped my briefcase, stopped in my tracks, and buried my head in my hands, mumbling an expletive or two, the result of frustration from an overwhelming day that hadn't even begun. Another thing to add to the list. A birthday gift for a man I'd barely spoken with since the day I'd escaped his tyrannical rule and driven off to college twenty-two years earlier.

As I dropped each child off one by one, a sense of shame grew, and the guilty feelings about the inconvenience of my father's birthday overwhelmed my spirit. Pulling the truck into a vacant parking lot I sobbed uncontrollably, ashamed not only about the behavior of the moment, but for all that I'd shown toward my dad since the day I left home. More than two decades earlier, I had declared my freedom from a kind of parental control that created hateful feelings no adolescent boy should have toward his father. Despite the aura of resentment that fixed itself between us, I craved his approval for the longest, until my own confidence reached a place where I no longer needed his. There is an inevitable volatility with a decision not to want, or need, your dad.

I'd heard the same voice once before two years earlier when it abruptly awakened me in the middle of the night in a cold sweat so profuse the sheets and pillow were soaked.

I want you to go tell your father about me, and I want you to do it now.

It was clear and precise. And it was two o'clock in the morning.

It was the last thing I ever expected to hear from God, who'd pretty much let me chart my own course when it came to spiritual growth and getting to know him better. Or so I believed at the time. Suddenly, in the strangest moment, He was prompting me to action so far outside my comfort zone I could barely breathe.

But he was placing this squarely upon my shoulders. So odd that God was calling me to action, and to help a man who had been so much about the fear and control of my youth. I never felt so much loved by my father as owned or possessed, like tractors and tools in a farm shop.

Two years earlier, I'd managed to fight off that undeniable voice. There is nothing so torturous to one's soul as telling God "no." But this time he would not be ignored. God called that day and he presented no detour off the path. Maybe it was all part of the plan.

A grand realization suddenly and gently poured into my spirit.

It was unbearable thinking I might be separated from my own father for eternity.

I called the office and canceled every appointment.

Why is it the most strenuous conversations and stressful circumstances take such an onerous place in our relationships with the people we love most, especially when everyone's trying to do the right thing? It is a great mystery.

Dad always struggled with self-worth and faith. Around 1995, I'd just begun the lifelong process of understanding mine. Despite the freedom in it all, and the fact that I'd taken up membership in a denomination with a strong emphasis on evangelism, I was unpracticed and uneasy at one-on-one conversations about God. It didn't help that Dad and I had an empty record of even the slightest casual conversation during the last twenty years. It made what felt like a divine calling all the more powerful.

This was real. A holy moment with a choice.

I'd purchased a copy of Randy Alcorn's *Heaven* just to get our conversation started. It's a great book that ponders answers to some of our most basic questions about eternity. Unwrapping the gift paper, and as he got his first glimpse of the cover, Dad held it with both hands and just stared not saying a word. You could almost see a tragically burdened spirit in surrender. He couldn't even raise his head.

"Thank you, son."

"You're welcome. I wanted to tell you some things I thought about this book, and some things I feel like I've experienced." It felt as if something, or someone, was almost speaking for me now that I'd taken a step.

"Okay." He placed the gift aside on his worn-out couch and looked at me like a real person for the first time in decades. "I'd like to hear that."

Somewhere in another realm, maybe close, or maybe very far away, God, in that moment, opened a door. My spirit sensed that very thing. The uneasiness and the tension never disappeared from the conversation, but it now channeled somehow differently.

For the next three hours Dad and I talked — the way fathers and sons actually should speak with one another. I told him about a certain peace I'd come to know pursuing a greater knowledge about God. I told him about forgiveness, and tried my best to describe its place in God's economy.

"I just think I've done too much," he said. "I haven't been a very good person."

"Well, neither have I, but I really believe God forgives me anyway."

And at that moment I asked what seemed the scariest question I'd ever asked another person — something I'd never done with anyone, and surely not with my own father.

"Do you want to pray with me?

"Yes, I'd like to do that," his answer surprisingly immediate and sure.

Instinctively, I took a deep breath.

I said the words and Dad repeated after me. We asked God to forgive our every mistake. Neglect. Anger. Excessive habits. Pride. Everything. We said we'd had a change of mind, and wished for a change in direction. *Metanoia*, it's called in the ancient scriptures. And at the very end, we sealed it all by telling God we believed he forgave us because that's his promise to a repentant heart.

At the end of those three hours we both looked like hell, as if we'd been through some bloody wartime battle. But we hugged, cried, and laughed. It was the most genuine moment I'd ever shared with my father. And obeying that voice felt like complete liberation, not the cloud of guilt I'd felt in the disobedience of twenty years before. It's the way a rehabilitated eagle must feel the moment it's released back into the wild — free to soar, and doing what it was meant to do.

I walked out of that old tool shop feeling victory as never before, almost like a hero.

There was no indication whatsoever how much warfare was still ahead, and how much God had yet to teach us about his timing, our failures, and His grace.

CHAPTER 2

Gut Gravity

*We are all strangers in a strange land, longing for home,
but not quite knowing what or where home is. We glimpse
it sometimes in our dreams, or as we turn a corner, and
suddenly there is a strange, sweet familiarity that vanishes
almost as soon as it comes.*

Madeleine L'Engle

I have never known what to call it, but it happens every year. Something that feels as core to my identity as the need to write, or the way I feel when I see my mother. As early as February each new year, a couple of days will come one after the other, portending winter's end. You know it's not true, but the soft winter sun stirs your blood reminding you how good it feels on your face, and the air so fresh it breathes like silk. For the first time in a long time your bones aren't cold.

After the long months of living in a dormant, brown country-side, you can smell the restless winter awaken, peeking momentarily into spring. You let it go because you know the Old Man will curl up and turn over for a few more weeks tomorrow. But the day is coming soon, and you will respond just as you have every other year before.

With these signs, I need to get my hands dirty and put something in the ground that will grow. Sweet hyacinths in the flower bed perhaps, or better yet, new spring potatoes in my back-yard, city-boy garden plot. It is this nostalgic sensation, this yearning each year, that lets me know I'm alive, and that I come from somewhere real. Hands in the soil inevitably speak, "Welcome home, farm boy. Good seeing you again."

It was my grandmother, our long-time family matriarch, who first told me about this kinship we have with the Arkansas delta dirt. Even in the days of her most debilitating arthritis, that old woman would get down on hands and knees because her soul would never rest if she wasn't putting things in the ground she could tend throughout spring. Her aged hands curled around it somehow, she could turn more dirt with a dull, worn-out butcher knife than a young man with a small John Deere tractor and a breaking plow. "This is what we do," she said. "The land is in our blood."

I remember this feeling as early as seven years old, taking the leftover seeds from my parents' annual vegetable garden, and planting a small patch I could tend for myself between two pecan trees in a field near home. There are few years I've missed since. There is nothing that satisfies a weary country spirit like putting seeds into the ground and helping something live.

This is a farm family's legacy. Simple. Unassuming. Authentic. Children of the dirt. We come from it. It is said we will return to it.

After twenty long years, I drove away from it without a second thought for another three decades.

There are two things that have shaped my life more than any other. One is the roller-coaster attitude toward the land of my youth, and the agrarian lifestyle we lived. As a boy and a young teen, it was a place of toil and sweat — the flat, barren, undramatic landscape where we assumed a monotonous tractor-driving job every day, and one that I came to loathe. As an older adult, it is a deeper understanding that appreciates and remembers the tough times a farm can bring, but also the colorful, story-rich life it availed. The kind an anxious boy is far too young to understand.

The other is the more complex relationship of growing up a farmer's son during the 1980s, the toughest time rural America saw since the Great Depression. This, much complicated by the fact that Dad was a man who loved fun more than work, drinking beer more than discovering truth (or telling the truth for that matter), and an absolute, unrestrained freedom that made him inwardly self-destructive and outwardly plain mean. For the longest time, I viewed my father and the rural homeland indistinguishably, and despised both.

But it's a restless life for someone who inwardly chases the ghost of approval from the same things he tells himself are outwardly unimportant.

CHAPTER 3

Numbing

We can easily forgive a child who is afraid of the dark; the real tragedy of life is when men are afraid of the light.

Plato

What evolved into both resentment and conflict avoidance in most of my immediate adult relationships began early in childhood as fear. A fourth-grade basketball coach who saw my early potential reinforced every insecurity he could with a daily insult.

"I wish someone would give me permission to slap you every five minutes just to make you meaner," he said frequently. "Whatever makes you so timid is keeping you at half your potential."

It's just about the worst thing you can say to a ten-year-old kid in a group of boys who already believe they're men.

Thirty years later, a nineteen-year marriage ended mostly because the verbal conflict terrified me, and I just didn't want to fight.

That fear of failure and conflict permeated most of my first fifty years.

It's the first thing I remember about him, that fear, and the sense that what my father most wanted, was precisely that — to instill and invoke fear, which he called discipline. And it was perplexing emotionally, because even at four years old, I knew I was supposed to love him, and it wasn't supposed to be hard.

His preferred beer made him sluggish, inattentive, and distracted. But the rare occasions when the whiskey came out produced an altogether different man.

It was 7 PM, the sun gradually fading as he extra-carefully maneuvered his Ford pickup off the road and into the driveway. We hadn't seen him for a good ten hours. In the time he'd been absent, one of the most violent spring storms we'd ever seen passed through northeast Arkansas and wreaked havoc on our home place, cotton trailers strewn about like toys and tree limbs shattered like so many icicles. We didn't know if he was dead or alive. His inexplicable absence through the afternoon Mom and I spent huddled together in a closet revealed itself quickly.

Mom met him at the door, almost reliving the panic from the tornado we'd experienced four hours earlier.

"Where have you been?" she begged hopelessly. "We could've died today, and for all we knew you were dead."

The stupefied look of a defenseless drunkard came across his face immediately. "What in hell are you talking about?"

"A tornado passed through here today," she implored.

"I ain't heard nothing about it," he slurred.

"My God, how drunk are you?" she said, tears now flowing.

Without a word, he turned and walked to the front of the house taking a seat on the front porch steps. A clay flower pot with red geraniums crashed as he fell to a seat.

Instinctively, Mom closed both the screen door and wooden door where we normally entered from the garage. Then she did something I'd never seen. She locked both.

With us locked inside, Dad sat alone on the front porch a good thirty minutes, the sun quickly setting, and my anxiety about the standoff now rising. He just sat there alone as if contemplating a story for the first time all day.

His boot steps echoed through the garage as he finally made his way back toward the locked doors.

The screen door jarred back and forth against the lock latch, softy first, then with stronger force.

"Open this damn door!" the violent shaking now rattling the door's top storm window. "I mean open it right now!" Mom sat at the kitchen bar staring blankly almost as if she knew what would come next.

More shaking and finally a loud noise of the door handle flying apart and metal pieces falling on concrete. His key would open the next door.

He now stood in the open doorway, screen door in hand pulled from its latch and torn from its hinges, ripped right off the frame. "I'll be damned if you lock me out of my own house," the words were barely discernible.

The screaming and yelling lasted for hours. From my room toward the back of our house I prayed they'd both be alive the next morning.

A lifetime of questions, soul-searching, and self-analysis will follow a man whose childhood was spent, half with contempt toward his father, and the other half desperately chasing his love and approval. It's easy blaming others for how you feel. But it's a whole different story going deeper, looking at things from everyone's point of view, considering all the circumstances, and realizing you're not always the completely innocent son you'd almost actually convinced yourself to see.

This book is a story about some of the deepest feelings a person can feel, especially those unique to fathers and sons, and the precious time wasted in estrangement toward the people we love most. There will always be something about sons and an innate desire to make their fathers proud. There will almost as often be something about imperfect fathers that disappoints their sons immensely — at least it seems that way in the South. I struggled with the two for almost fifty years, and much because of my own shortcomings let the latter win out more often that it should. David Watkins was a fun-loving country boy some moments. An insecure tyrant in others, with behavior as unpredictable as the July rains. That's how the eighties affected farmers. I let those feelings about him tarnish everything I could possibly associate with him — farming, family, and especially the community we called home. All were despised by association. He seemed so perfectly at peace driving those country roads, drinking beer, smoking Winstons, and loafing at the local hideaways. Most all I ever thought about was getting away from him, and leaving that place forever.

But it's also a story much about the healing nature of time and circumstance, and the reality that as we look more thoughtfully at the complex relationships of the past, we see that everyone pretty much does the best they can do with what they've been given. Fathers, sons, mothers, daughters. None of this is easy business.

And there is a wonderful evolution about it all that shapes our personalities and who we become as we manage the imperfect family tree. It is a story about place, and culture, and a rural kind of life that almost no longer exists. It is fueled by people — good people, I have come to understand.

My father and the amazing agricultural landscape we called home were the two things that put both the color and the character into my life. When a deputy sheriff calls at 10 P M and tells you that you need to come get your fifty-five-year-old father out of jail because he just got in a tussle with a local cop, you're qualified to claim a colorful life. In time, you can even laugh about it.

On the days I miss my father most — those days when I wish we could just sit on the porch and share a cold drink and watch the purple martins he loved so much — I often take a short drive. It's no more than an hour away. I go back to the place where it all happened and I find myself cruising the country roads just as he did. I see hands on the steering wheel and they are my father's worn and age-spotted hands. I pass the very spot on the old home place where he surprised me one oppressive July morning, breaking out in an a cappella baritone rendition of *Swing Low, Sweet Chariot*. Cruising down the river levee, I recall the adrenaline of early winter mornings as we'd head for the St. Francis River and the prospect of a mallard duck limit seasoned with lots of tall tales. Yes, time and understanding have made things better. Or maybe it's the unthinkable.

Perhaps I've become my father's son.

Some days now I long for that life we lived on Highbanks Road. And I thank God for the promise that He never gets angry with people like me or my dad for being who we are.

CHAPTER 4

The King Is Crowned

Even though it is more blessed to give than to receive, sometimes you need to be the object of someone else's compassion.

J. Earp

In 1971, the United States ratified the 26th Amendment to the Constitution giving eighteen-year-olds the right to vote, the New York Times published the Pentagon Papers exposing how many young lives were lost in a war found mostly to be a lie, and a man named Walt Disney opened a theme park he called Disney World in the middle of the Florida swamps. It took fifteen rounds, but Joe Frazier bested Muhammed Ali in the Fight of the Century, and legendary artist John Denver released a forever classic called *Take Me Home, Country Roads.*

Not quite so prominently broadcast amongst the headlines was a once-in-a-lifetime opportunity that freed David Watkins from the factory assembly line for a life where he would become master of his own domain.

Whatever its source, there is something about abuse and control that will send any soul into a rebellion. We will purge the poison that smothers that soul, else it will linger and fester forever until we find a place where we perceive freedom. Now on his own with the place where he was raised far behind, and where he could put a mindful distance between him and his father, my dad had landed a blue-collar job polishing brass bathroom fixtures on an assembly line. But the day-in, day-out, clock-in, clock-out, managed by a dozen layers of administrative bureaucracy only made him hunger more for the freedom he saw outside an eight-hour second shift with two weeks' holiday pay per year. And he lived in a place where he was surrounded by pickup trucks and tractors and families reaping the benefits of the early 1970s agricultural heyday.

In January 1971, David Watkins found both his freedom and his livelihood, and he never looked back. Whether he ever realized or appreciated the uncommon good fortune that allowed it was something he never discussed.

The thing about becoming a cotton farmer is that it's not a vocation you choose to pursue one night, and stand in line for an interview with your resume and application in hand the next. Cotton farms are capital-intensive entrepreneurial enterprises requiring land and equipment, both of which are expensive, the land with ownership so protected it often gets passed through as many as six to seven generations. That's how strongly people identify with their land. Like a family with claim to the throne, most young men pay their dues for years on their father's farm before moving from glorified hired hand to rookie farmer. Farmers don't choose their work. They are *born into* it.

So it was some incredible good fortune when his mother-in-law offered a two hundred-acre inheritance her nephew farmed for a decade and give it to Dad as a startup for a small operation that would launch him into freedom and new life. He never became Craighead County's Farmer of the Year, but in January 1971, David Watkins got his farm and he found his freedom. It wasn't the last time an act of extraordinary generosity would turn his life around.

By comparison to neighbors and friends, he was a small operator in those early years. His tractors were used, each with several hundred hours on the meter. There was a one-row cotton picker, and some rusty four-row equipment that prepared the seed beds. But his peripheral vision was blind to comparison. He was free.

The biggest bonus? Harvest ended just in time for duck season. It was his greatest delight, and shortcoming, as a farmer. He viewed those three to four months between harvest and spring planting as vacation. Between duck and quail hunting, cruising dirt roads with a cooler full of beer, and other generalized loafing activities, he was a man of leisure, so exhausted by each day's experience that he was almost always into a full snore on the living room sofa every afternoon by four. There were a million pre-season and pro-active jobs a farmer could take on in the off-season — new points on the plows, changing cotton picker spindles, new knives and guards on the combine header. But he loved the leisure side of his life too much for pro-activity. It was almost as if he could never quench his long thirst for independence.

CHAPTER 5

Duck Woods

There are moments when all anxiety and stated toil are
becalmed in the infinite leisure and repose of nature.
                                            Henry David Thoreau

Wherever you find water flowing through fields of grain for thousands of miles you'll find something special — one of nature's greatest manifestations. More than three hundred twenty-five bird species make the round trip each year along the Mississippi River Flyway from their breeding grounds in Canada and the northern U.S. to wintering grounds along the Gulf of Mexico, some as far south as Patagonia. Forty percent of all North American migrating waterfowl follow the route annually. These ecosystems come together in the Delta flatlands between the St. Francis and Mississippi Rivers creating a sportsman's paradise. Most kids in these parts grow up thinking a duck blind is their second home. Many are as nice as one.

If you want to know the weather forecast from November through January, turn the television off and set down your smartphone. Just look to the sky. The mallard ducks and Canada geese will give you days' advance notice of a major weather pattern shift. Some days the V-shaped flight patterns extend north to south twisting and turning as far as the eye can see. For the locals, it's a sight as comforting and nostalgic as beans and ham hock on a cold winter's day. The flight is on.

When he wasn't in the duck blind, my dad would sit at a bedroom window for hours, binoculars pointed to the river just a mile and a half west. Duck hunters dream of that magical day when there are so many ducks you can't keep them off your pond, and the steel of your gun barrel stays hot, no time between rounds.

In those days, you'd find dozens of pickup trucks scattered about Highbanks Landing and the more northerly Jackson's Landing, hunters having gathered for boat launches oftentimes long before there was enough light to maneuver the tricky river runs. Most could navigate by memory, jumping one log after another and dodging brush along the way. Shooting hours began precisely at sun up and mallards move early for the day's first feeding. Run a boat to your blind late between prime shooting hours of six and nine in the morning and you might just find it unplugged and half sunk at the landing tomorrow morning. One of the first rules on the St. Francis River is respect for the other guy.

If you've never been there, if you've never felt the adrenaline rush that overpowers you when twenty-five mallard ducks decide they're coming into your pond, it goes something like this.

Three hundred yards out, a spotter first sees them headed due north. The blind's designated chief caller, oftentimes an old river veteran in his fifties or sixties, makes his way to the shooting window as he reaches into a camouflaged vest pocket for his long caller. The call, maybe a black P.S. Olt, or a smooth, synthetic Rich-N-Tone, is doubly secured around the caller's neck with a lengthy cord adorned with duck bands from past hunts. The bands, likely placed around the bird's leg in the northern nesting grounds, are a research and reporting tool effective only when the hunter harvests the duck and returns the band to the research organization. Many prefer wearing the bands like an Indian bead necklace, each representing the memories of a past hunt and signifying their place within the tribe.

The chief caller takes a deep breath bringing the mouthpiece to his lips and the hopeful long call begins. The long call has a rhythm. A series of loud duck-like calls that grow shorter and closer together as the caller manages his breath with as much perfection as a first-chair trombonist. Almost like a plea of sorts, the long call is loud and imprecise, designed only to get the attention of ducks moving at a distance. Get their attention, and maybe they'll like what they see. They'll assess the wind, the pond configuration, decoy pattern, water clarity, and other factors before moving on or breaking for a descent. If he gets their attention, the caller then has a "working" bunch of ducks. Things are serious now, and the beauty of a seasoned caller unfolds.

Instinctively, the mood changes. Hunters give a quick check to their Brownings, Winchesters, and Remingtons. Safety on. Chamber full. Locked and loaded.

There is anticipation in this critical moment when it's important to read what's happening outside the blind. It takes years to get really good at this. The chief caller and the spotters now work together watching the ducks work the pond, their necks twisting and turning out the shooting window. The calling changes, now

more intentional, more precise, as the ducks assess everything around them and make a final decision about a water landing. This is the moment a seasoned duck caller shows his skill alternating between working calls. There are calls to get the ducks' attention, others that lure them in, feeding chatters, and a "come back" call for those that want to move on. The pros give the ducks exactly what they want to hear. This can go on thirty minutes or more, and callers frequently become so short on breath they find themselves light-headed.

There is not a memory from childhood more vivid than the clarity of my father's eyes as he worked a bunch of mallard ducks on a freezing cold St. Francis River day. In those moments, all self-consciousness, issues of self-worth, all his imperfections vanished. Fluid, at ease, and seasoned with experience, he demonstrated complete control, perfect peace.

The call is reduced to the occasional soft chatter now. This is what separates the great duck callers from the good ones. A great duck caller knows when to call, and when to be quiet. Then, it's in that quiet moment you first hear it. They're coming in right over the blind. If Dad said it once in that thrilled whisper, he said it a million times. *Grab your guns, boys. Get 'em on three ...*

You hear them before you see them, and the sound is unmistakable. Once a four-pound mallard duck commits to landing on water there is no turning back. With feet extended, body bowed, and wings cupped, the ducks flap wings violently for a soft landing. As they do, the wind whistles across long feathers in increasingly quick repetition. *Shew-shew-shew-shew-shew.* All movement in the blind ceases and you can hear a pin drop. *Guns up. One, two, three!*

The purest sportsmen will set their gun sights and pull triggers just before the ducks hit the water. Some prefer allowing the ducks to land, giving them even more time and accuracy for a maximum harvest. Either way, there's not a moment more thrilling than the sound of wind over wings. It's rare, but on the good days this scenario may play out six or seven times. They are the days you recount to your grandchildren.

David Watkins was always afraid he'd miss that day. One day, the pursuit took a radical turn.

The ducks were moving slowly that day and the prospects for any action were slim. Dad had an unusual restlessness about him, especially for this place where he was usually so content.

What I remember most is how much helpless thinking time there was between the moment we got the news, and the time we learned the truth. I was a seven-year-old kid, bystander to a sudden and dramatic conversation indicating my mother might be dead. The hours of uncertainty ahead were sickening.

About ten o'clock that morning, Dad got the urge for a change of scenery and we motored from our normal duck blind deep into the woods thinking we might find a feeding frenzy. Sonny Schug, known as one of the Dixie Boys, had a small blind in those deep woods and as we motored into his pond he invited us to join him and pick up a pocket full of heat from his propane stove. Hunting from a new blind was always an adventure. With the change of scenery, you just knew the ducks would pour in. Sportsmen, if nothing else, are eternal optimists.

A few bunches came and passed us by, and the hunt turned to more of a social visit between Dad and Sonny. Sonny was a well-established farmer, his operation only five or six miles from ours as the crow flies across the river, though it was a twenty-five-mile drive.

In the far-away distance we heard a boat motoring closer. Occasionally, someone yelled out, and the longer it went on the more clearly we could hear it was my father's name being called. Another ten minutes passed and Mack Pitts, a young outdoorsman my father loved like a son, motored straight to the blind's shooting window.

"David, are you in there?" he asked, his voice almost trembling.

"Mack," dad replied, "what the hell are you doing this deep in the woods?"

"It's Margaret. She's had a stroke."

Dad's facial expression went from carefree to bewildered in an instant. For a few moments, there was a silent confusion and he seemed more frustrated than concerned.

"What?"

"Margaret. Everyone's been looking for you. They've got her in the hospital."

No longer looking at Dad, I thought my life had just changed forever.

Dad was now preoccupied, but never seemed overly worried. With Mom at a hospital forty minutes from home, we had an hour-long boat ride from the deep woods to the landing, a fifteen-minute drive home, then on to the hospital. Guns unloaded and coats zipped, we stepped down into the boat. "Hang on extra strong," he zipped my life jacket. "We're gonna move," he said.

For the next hour, he pushed a 9.9 horsepower Mercury outboard as hard as it would go. Weaving our way through the narrow runs, dodging limbs, and jumping sunken cypress logs there was nothing I could do but clinch the seat and think. *My mother is dying, there's nothing I can do about it, and I may live alone with this man the rest of my life.*

The pickup truck spun its wheels and gravel flew as we tore away from Jackson's Landing. He dropped me at my grandmother's just a few miles down the road and short of our home. Again, nothing but time and morbid uncertainty ahead. I went to bed dreading the next morning's news and prayed to God my mom would live.

There weren't a lot of cardiologists practicing medicine in rural Arkansas during the early eighties. The diagnosis required several trips to Memphis, but Mom had not experienced a stroke. Instead, she had a defective heart valve that exhibited a few stroke-like symptoms. With medication, she'd be okay.

Recounting the story of his hospital arrival years later, she remained astounded that he'd taken two hours at home getting ready, then strolled to a restaurant for a nice lunch within fifteen minutes of his hospital arrival.

All I cared about was the assurance Mom was coming home.

CHAPTER 6

Deafening Silence

Love isn't complicated, people are.

unknown

The first real lessons I remember learning about things like truth, love, obedience, and grace weren't found in a church or a book. Neither were they related from a preacher's sermon or a teacher's lesson. They came from a drunken and violent father who cursed my mother and wanted me to lie for him two to three times a week.

Why my father decided he'd pick me up from school that 1976 winter season was always a mystery, and so unlike him, but it was nice looking out the classroom window each afternoon just before the three o'clock bell rang, seeing his pickup truck and knowing he was there. Maybe it was easy for me using the situation and pretending even momentarily that we had some great father-son relationship — or even a normal one. It was comforting thinking so in the moment, even knowing the high odds of the coming reality.

Whether he'd been drinking or not was discernible at a distance, even to a ten-year-old kid. After two beers, the sharpness in his eyes disappeared and you could see a certain numbness in his facial features. When he wasn't drinking, Daddy was clear-eyed, handsome, and deliberate in every movement, every word. He had a commanding presence and spoke like thunder. But the drinking visibly altered everything about him, rapidly reducing him from commanding to pathetic. It only took a fraction of a second opening the pickup truck door to confirm the fear. The farm truck cab reeked of cigarette smoke and alcohol.

What happened next was predictable, and gut wrenching.

Mom's routine 4:45 P M arrival home from teaching each day gave him almost two hours from the time he picked me up to drink, smoke, and cruise the dirt roads before his evening ritual that always began with passing out on the couch before supper. As we cruised the countryside not even talking really, he'd guzzle a six-pack one by one — tossing his just-emptied can out the window and into the road ditch then reaching for the next lukewarm beer stowed beneath the driver's seat. He kept his habit hidden underneath that truck seat, a place so obvious I never understood why he even went to the trouble. Inside the musty cab coated with tobacco tar and farm dust six months old, the cigarette smoke got so thick my irritated eyes burned and streamed stinging tears. Public service announcements about second-hand smoke were still a few years ahead, though it likely wouldn't have mattered. Eventually I'd timidly ask permission to crack a window. Five minutes later he'd complain we were letting cold air in, and the suffocation resumed.

That wasn't even close to the worst of it.

Sitting in that passenger seat riding aimlessly across the countryside watching my dad drink and smoke seemed the biggest waste of time. There were a million better, more productive things we could pursue, and surely many that would produce less conflict. It would have been nice to share time shooting some hoops. I don't think it ever crossed his mind to dedicate some father-son time to teaching me about mechanics or how to take apart, clean, and put a shotgun back together.

And the conflict was coming sure as the world. But first, the familiar fear.

By 4:30 P M we'd routinely make our way toward home, heading west on Highbanks Road. The county paved the road that year, transforming country gravel into smooth passage but minus any yellow lines. It was just plain black pavement. As a bonus, they'd dug the drainage ditches on each side nice and deep. After a six pack in the truck and somewhere around his eighth beer for the afternoon, my dad was drunk enough that he'd swerve to and fro heading home. There were always one or two occasions on the two-mile stretch homeward when the tires veered off the pavement onto the gravel shoulder coming perilously within inches of the ditch. He almost always veered right and never left. That's something you remember from a passenger's point of view.

I'd instinctively pull my body toward the middle of the bench seat bracing for impact just as he'd jerk the wheel left, correcting near calamity. The frightening thought of going headfirst into the ditch was surpassed only by the embarrassment I'd feel from the next person who came along and became obliged to hook on a chain and pull us out. No son ever wants to see another man pity his father.

Forty years later, nightmares about those unsettling moments still haunt my sleep.

Even in the rural country, people talked, and you never quite looked at a family the same again after its leader got found drunk in a ditch. It's heavy stuff for a kid. Even as we'd make it to our driveway without incident, there was still the moment ahead when Mom got home and she'd know he'd been drinking just as quickly as I had back in the school yard.

The inevitable argument between them was always preceded by my dad's consistently stern, if drunken, warning just before we'd walk into the house. He'd look me dead in the eye and spit out the slurred admonishment.

"Don't you tell your mama I been drinking. If she asks you, say no." He must have said it a hundred times, and I don't think I ever acknowledged it or replied once. Ignoring him was the safest rebellion I could muster short of him doing something unpredictably violent. Serving as a pawn between two parents tormented my young spirit, and the thought of lying to Mom made me sick. Oftentimes, I'd pray he'd fall asleep in the ten minutes before she'd arrive.

I stayed quiet a lot, but I never once lied to my mother. It wasn't even a thing to contemplate.

Even a fourth grader has instincts about right and wrong within the family. Children may not understand the psychology and behaviorism behind one person luring another into their complicit web, but a young person knows when his stomach churns because something feels so wrong. That one parent consistently commanded a lie on his behalf to the other — it was soul-crushing and kept me up at night. I remember praying for peace and something normal in my parents' relationship.

He was the kind of man so caught up in the present moment and how circumstances affected him and oblivious to all others, he could do decades worth of damage in a single sentence. The peripheral vision of his emotional sensitivities was legally blind.

Their worst arguments from the day before would resume around five o'clock the next day over their morning coffee. From the bedroom and under the covers, I oftentimes heard tensions escalate to the point when my father would back himself into a verbal corner and, having nothing else to defend himself, spew hate toward my mom. His words are still some of the most devastating I've heard in a lifetime.

"You go to hell," he frequently countered, and his blue eyes appeared as cold fire. Alone in a dark bedroom, horrific images ran through my mind. A kid should never have the picture of such a hopeless thought painted for him. It seemed they were outright enemies.

Hours later at school, I could almost erase the memory by noon, but soon I was back to wondering which of the three likely scenarios would play out that evening. It offered scarce time for peace of mind. Imagining the night ahead was mentally exhausting.

Preferably, my parents would pretend nothing ever happened and we'd all move on with life until next time — there would always be a next time. Sweeping it all under the rug was a great relief, but it was just buying time. The bickering might pick up where it left off, so I'd go back to my room and try not hearing it. Or the worst case, there would be silence. It might go on for an evening, or maybe for several days. The prolonged silence between my parents sometimes made me physically ill.

In all the arguments, my mom never asked a single time for confirmation that my dad drank, nor did she ask me to lie. It may be the most gracious gesture of love anyone ever showed me.

But children who grow up fearing conflict will run from it the rest of their lives. This, I learned on my own.

The volatility in my parents' marriage had an unusual impact on my youthful aspirations, and nearly fifty years later, the things I still view as most important in life today. My boyhood dreams were not those of becoming a cowboy, an astronaut, or a policeman. Instead, I dreamed of family, mostly a loving wife with whom I shared a magical, mutual adoration — two people in love who couldn't get enough of each another. There was peace and contentment, and above all, commitment to a relationship where the threat of its end never entered the picture. And I spent my entire adolescence and early adulthood chasing that dream hard. So hard, in fact, that in such a hurry to be happy and see the dream play out, I envisioned every young woman I dated as the one with whom I'd live out that fairy tale. In the end, my rushed first marriage lasted for nineteen years, but caused me to wonder if I was a worse man than my father had ever been.

Ask me about growing up on Highbanks Road and I could share stories for hours. I will tell you how much I despised it and laid blame upon it. In the next breath, I will tell you how the lessons of tragedy and wounds of youth ultimately get put in perspective. And how they eventually help you to know that people don't necessarily have to understand one another to love one another.

Mostly, I will tell you *it's complicated.*

CHAPTER 7

A Land That Lived

My wound is geography. It is also my anchorage, my port of call.

Pat Conroy

A person never thinks much about the beauty or soul of a place where they've spent so much time — that is until they've been absent from it a good long while. There is something about time and grace, almost like a gold miner's pan, that washes away what once was worthless and despised, and now leaves behind only the richest nuggets of goodness and fondness of heart.

It may have been the least pretentious place on earth.

Highbanks Road was one of those places where you spent considerable time thinking about everywhere, or anywhere else, you could possibly be outside northeast Arkansas. Dreaming from a weathered, threadbare lawn chair, even at seven years old I'd frequently spend the waning hours of each summer afternoon gazing westward as a fiery dusk backlit zig-zagging jet contrails in all directions. They brought an out-of-place geometric quality to the heavenly sky, otherwise painted with soft crisscrossing brush strokes seemingly from God's own hand, and with marvelous colors that didn't have a name. But each contrail invited its own wonderment to another world so far away.

It was a childhood rush contemplating who was going where in those jets, and the adventure ahead for each passenger. The travelers inside were surely a cosmopolitan lot. You could almost see them sipping champagne from tall glasses and tasting caviar with tiny spoons. Were they looking out the window in my direction? Did world-traveling adventurers like them ever think about dirt farmers like us? Those evening skies painted a wonder of possibilities offering hope and distraction at the same time.

But at the end of those imaginary adventures was a sudden, sometimes depressing reality. Come morning, our providence had us bound for a clod-ridden, gumbo field.

It was the quiet end of an era that farm folks dreaded so long it practically went unnoticed when it happened, although no one can pinpoint exactly when that was. But around the same time the Berlin Wall fell across an ocean divide, an honorable and uniquely American lifestyle more than a century old slipped away, a reality only in the history books now. The rural families who worked the small Delta cotton farm vanished, victim to high costs, low returns, and a government that practically forgot the American small farmer, forcing them to go big or go home. For so many, there was no good option.

If a kid wanted to know more about a world outside cotton farming, he watched television — shows like *The Undersea World of Jacques Cousteau*, or *Big Blue Marble*, or even the Olympics.

Or he spent time with books. A thirty-two volume set of Funk & Wagnalls encyclopedias occupied two full summers of reading time. Everywhere between the covers of those books seemed so distantly far away, places like Zimbabwe and Caracas and the Caribbean Sea. And I spent considerable time dreaming about going to each one. There is a sanguine chasm between the two — being somewhere and dreaming of going there. It filled me with both angst and hope.

I imagined every day what it would be like to someday just get up and go and never look back. And in time, I started planning that day.

There are no directional signs pointing you to Highbanks Road. None for that matter even identifying it by name. It's never been much of a destination, but more of a place you had to go to get somewhere else. For twenty-odd years it was landmarked only by a misspelled sign pointing the way to Macey Cemetary (sic). Either no one noticed the misspelling, or just as likely, no one cared.

In rural Arkansas, front porches are made for hand-churned ice cream, shelling purple hull peas by the bushel, and drinking glasses of sweet iced tea so cold the condensation forms rivulets against the stifling humidity. Some pass their Sunday afternoons perusing *Garden & Gun* magazine while others are glued to NASCAR or the latest televised tournament on the bass fishing circuit. Here, the celebrity power of Bill Dance or Jimmy Houston trumps Lady Gaga every time. It's a place where your beer cooler's brand name is almost as much a matter of pride as what you call your bird dog. In a pinch, you can generally find a pretty good chicken gizzard dinner at the gas station. And it's the kind of community that when someone sees Old Lady Hout in the general store wearing pajamas, they don't say a word because they respect her for the educational pioneer she once was, not for what her failing mind has become.

Highbanks Road is a three-mile east-to-west passage out in the country, bookended by Arkansas Highway 139 and the St. Francis River, dead ending into the muddy waters flowing along the western edge of the heart of the old Macey Community. The now-shuttered beer joints of the Missouri Bootheel and Red Onion community once thrived just north. It's unremarkable and undistinguished, a few homesteads along the way, most dotting the corners of forty-acre cotton fields, their homes appointed abundantly with enough preserved dead animal parts to launch a small PETA riot. But those twelve-point bucks, eight-pound bass, and a couple of extra-long turkey beards mounted against cheap, polished oak above the mantels tell stories as rich as William Faulkner ever knew.

County Road 514, as it became known in the progressive nineties, was a simple gravel thoroughfare maintained by the county road department. What that really meant was a monthly pass with a road grader, and you were sure-as-the-world bound to get a nail in your tire next trip to town, so the adults cussed every time the grader appeared knowing you'd have to spend money at Dean's Tire Store. Every time the grader passed stirring up old nails and railroad spikes, it pushed Dean's monthly revenues into the plus column. The grader driver had a big mustache and kept a big coffee Thermos in the cab. He looked so comfortable in the air-conditioned cab on those oppressive July mornings when I chopped cotton on our home place, and he'd creep by with the cringing noise of blade against rock. But he always waved. So I waved, too, but couldn't stop thinking about how hot I was and how cool he must feel.

Youth on the farm was so unfair in an indentured servant sort of way. I was grateful for every distraction, even if only momentary.

Rednecks frequently made their mark on Highbanks Road leaving behind pock-marked road signs after taking drunken target practice with handguns and .22 caliber rifles. Every sign on the road was shot up at least a half dozen times. For many, the drunker they got, the better their marksmanship, and the more self-impressed they became. Some thought it cheap Friday night entertainment. If the county sheriff's office cared, no one could tell.

The town drunk, Oscar Wiles, frequented High Banks Road in an old brown Ford Maverick. Old Oscar got drunk three times a week on whatever he could afford and you'd often find him in his car, passed out in a ditch snoring, tobacco juice running down his chin and onto a crusty shirt. Depending on the angle Oscar hit the ditch, at least one of the Maverick's balding tires was always suspended mid-air. People said Oscar never broke a bone because the booze loosened him up so much.

"Having trouble, Osc?" my dad would ask playfully as we pulled up on the scene. Oscar growled unintelligibly. "I'll be fine. Go on and get out of here," he'd growl some more.

Oscar had no preferences for his drinking times. Tuesday afternoon was just as good as Friday night. One Saturday, Oscar got so smashed he pulled off the road, up our driveway, and into the open garage where he passed out at the wheel for an hour. Mom was petrified, but even I knew he was harmless, and besides, he was about to distract my weekly viewing of Wide World of Sports, so I ignored him. It wasn't long until he cranked the engine and backed nearly fifty yards back down our driveway and onto the road as if it were just another day. He never looked back toward the road once.

We pulled him out from road ditches a hundred times if one. Oscar eventually died in an accident one night when he crashed into a ditch and the car went ablaze. Privately, people swore a local troublemaker came along and killed Oscar for sport, just as he was known to do with stray dogs. The thug was surely mean enough to make it a credible suspicion. He's now serving a life sentence in the Cummins Prison Unit for killing a couple and dumping their bodies in a drainage ditch. Many believe he was responsible for taking the lives of a half dozen or more people over the years.

The land's character flowed and transitioned with the seasons subtly, almost magically, in such a way the local residents payed it no mind at all. The drunkards who frequented it, many of them war veterans of extraordinary valor, others just lazy husbands temporarily escaping nagging wives, were too numb and too tired to see things like high-minded metaphors in the land.

Fortunes were, and still are made some years in the rich, alluvial soils of the forty-acre tracts extending north and south along that three-mile thoroughfare. Some fields near the river are nothing more than gumbo sloughs. Others are dotted with desert-like sand blows where over the centuries underground fissures trailing off the New Madrid fault push worthless dirt upward, dotting the landscape and robbing its consistent look of otherwise perfect and identical rows. But in most places, the soil composition is the ideal blend of sandy loam, that when married with forty-two inches of annual rainfall and an eight-month growing season, produces a decent living for the few dozen farm families who remain.

Drought, biblical-like insect plagues, hundred-year floods, and the rare fall hail storm have wiped out fourth-generation farm families in other years. Where the land is a community's life blood there is nothing more tragic than when a farm family goes under and an auctioneer chatters impalpably into a cheap, crackling microphone for hours gaveling one item after another SOLD. The spirits of our ancestors weep when it happens, or so we imagine. It is the blessing, and the curse, of family farmland stewardship. This responsibility, and its preservation for the next generation is all that really matters.

If you can't pass the land on to your children, all might as well be lost.

CHAPTER 8

His Kingdom

We say that flowers return every spring, but that is a lie. It is true that the world is renewed. It is also true that renewal comes at a price, for even if the flower grows from an ancient vine, the flowers of spring are themselves new to the world, untried and untested.

Daniel Abraham

It's the harvest season that brings out the thrill of living along Highbanks Road. Look to the sky in September and October for the free daily aerial acrobatics. The local daredevil crop dusters in single-engine planes swoop hair-raisingly low beneath the power lines then pull skyward before arching down and back like a pendulum for the next pass across quarter-mile fields preparing cotton and soybeans for harvest. Dad and I watched Tommy Adams crash upside-down and nose-first less than a hundred yards behind our house. He was spraying for army worms in a wheat field that May day. Tommy walked away, but died in another crash a month later. They said it was the trauma of the first crash that took his life in the second. He'd invited me up for my first airplane ride just two weeks earlier.

Early evenings around dusk you can see the countryside dotted with combines and cotton pickers moving slowly, but feverishly up and down quarter-mile rows across fields with signature names like Tiny's Forty, Turkey Run, Big Sandy, or the Keich Place down on the corner. The innovative farmers, who by necessity have tripled their yields in thirty years, are joyful bringing in the crop, but know they are one torrential rain away from a total loss. As the evening settles in, the machines become distant lights crawling across empty darkness backlit only by the occasional harvest moon. But there is a smooth, mechanical hum that blends in perfect unison like a choir across the countryside. You can smell the harvest, too. It is dusty and rich at the same time, nostalgic in such a way that it reminds folks this is their home.

If fall is its livelihood, it's winter that welcomes the Highbanks Road recreational season.

For two months each winter, sportsmen from across the countryside pull camouflaged boats and outboard motors behind four-wheel-drive pickup trucks toward the St. Francis River and Highbanks Landing lickety-split before sunup every morning. They are in search of mallard ducks where they hunt from the non-apologetically cozy confines of heated duck blinds appointed with old couches and tattered reclining chairs. Poor man's kingdoms, they are. Duck blinds get passed sacredly from one family generation to the next, most as treasured as granny's old cast iron frying pan. Old-timers know the river well enough they can tell who's doing the shooting just by listening. "Well, there goes Hog 'em. He's got 'em workin','" they'd say after a round of never-ending shotgun blasts.

"Crumpety Pump's at it again. We'll never hear the end of it at the coffee shop," they said, when a round echoed from the south.

"It's the Dixie Boys' day," Daddy said a hundred times, jealous as could be with us only a quarter mile east and down the river run.

Some loved hunting the muddy waters of the St. Francis River for sport. Others were just along for the fellowship and tall tales. A few sought undeserved respite from nagging wives who wished their husbands would do more productive things than hunt ducks, drink beer, and fall asleep on the couch, only to repeat the cycle the next day.

I never saw my father more at perfect peace than in the many hours he spent peering intently skyward through a musty burlap bag draped across our duck blind's shooting window. All the time he wasn't there was spent wishing that he was.

It was bad enough that our rural electric provider had a reputation for losing power every time the wind blew. But January 1976 brought an ice storm wrecking trees and power lines so badly the whole community closed for three weeks. They said it was the worst in forty years. Our family of three spent twenty-one days huddled around a fireplace, roasting marshmallows and cooking on an open fire, playing board games and gin rummy until cabin fever drove us practically mad. Mom and Dad, who both grew up without the convenience of indoor plumbing thought it a riot that at ten years old I had to learn how to relieve myself outside in subfreezing weather. You make all kinds of bodily adjustments when you're pooping in an eight-inch snow. Those three weeks may have been the best quality time we ever spent together as a family. I remember wishing it would never end.

Daddy took his four-wheel-drive pickup out for a drive every day "checking the roads." He was surely loafing and drinking coffee at Ball-Hout Implement tractor dealership escaping what Mom and I could not. Every day for ten days he offered the same ominous report. "Roads still too bad to get y'all out. It's slick as glass out there," he said, never once looking us in the eye.

When we finally loaded up for a family drive on the tenth day there was both wreckage we couldn't comprehend, and an ominous beauty we never expected.

One home place after another appeared ravaged, seventy-year-old oak and pecan trees shattered and power lines strewn everywhere, collapsed by seven inches of icy weight. Cars and trucks were left abandoned in ditches at least every quarter mile. The countryside was silent with inactivity. It was not a peaceful quiet. It was dead silence.

But every so often there was a contrast of hope. Dozens of farmers left their cotton stalks uncut that year, and the icy storm covered every inch of every branch. As the southerly sun's soft winter light gleamed through the clouds, the fields appeared as a brilliant farm of dazzling crystal jewels. A harvested cotton farm covered in ice during January qualifies as one of the world's incredible visual wonders.

Every spring on Highbanks Road brings another chance to get things right. Even after months spent fretting over crop disasters that brought some farm families to the brink of collapse, it's as if God erases the bad memories clean and puts a new spring in everyone's collective step. For farm folk, hope and faith are never more evident than watching a John Deere tractor pull a twelve-row cotton planter through the field on a sunny April day. There is something about the sweet smell of freshly turned Delta farmland and a tractor's diesel exhaust that makes all things new. It's almost as comforting as the crispy-fried hog jowl, black-eyed peas, and cornbread most families surely enjoyed weeks earlier for New Year's day lunch, this a long-time tradition of the culture, ensuring peace and prosperity in the growing season ahead.

Within a few weeks, the barren countryside evolves with life and character. Vivid redbuds, wild wisteria vines, and dogwood trees burst forth the first signs of color along muddy ditch banks where soft shell turtles, instinctive to the new season, line up by the dozens on floating logs, warming their cold blood in the sunshine. Old timers swear the dogwood blooms signal the first prospect of good spring crappie fishing on the St. Francis barrow pits.

Imagine a May day filled with bright sunshine, but cool enough that you want to breathe every breath so deep you can taste the sweet honeysuckle through the air. The red-winged blackbirds scour the roadside for anything left behind, and mourning doves and red-tailed hawks, natives naturally at odds, look down from power lines, fence posts, and whatever vantage point they can find.

Cotton, soybean, and corn seeds germinate, cracking through the crust reaching toward a seasonal sun now more directly overhead. In days, fields are transformed into familiar shades of green as tiny leaves unfurl exposing their vulnerability to the next sandstorm or hailstorm surely just ahead. For the next several weeks, rice farmers will never be more than a few steps away from rubber boots and a shovel. The levees never break conveniently after morning coffee and toast.

The farmers often think they'd be just as well off with an annual trip to Vegas laying everything they have on a single turn of the cards. Instead they follow a generational calling that builds another layer of character and toughness, each one telling a story like the rings of an ancient oak.

They will never be adorned with medals and ribbons pinned to their chests, nor will they set a salary record for a single season, but they will risk it all one year after another because of a calling so strong it's as if God, by His own hand, draws them to the soil.

The calendar reads that it's four months into the new year, but for the seasonally driven farm families along Highbanks Road, the year is just beginning.

The Arkansas Delta knows nothing about a gentle transition from spring to summer. One day in late May it's pleasant and folks are smiling. The next is so sultry your glasses fog. It's so oppressive the Methodist preacher swears under his breath, and the Baptist preacher wants to. Relief comes only with the occasional late-afternoon thunderheads that build ominously sky high until accumulating so much moisture they collapse with welcome rains. When the clouds part and the sun returns, the steaming ground will actually scald a young soybean plant to its early death.

In 1977, a young county judge made good on a campaign promise to pave Highbanks Road. That was an exciting prospect since I'd still not figured how to make use of the roller skates gifted by a Florida aunt the previous Christmas. The judge fulfilled half his promise. They shut the asphalt machines down after two miles, and the blacktop turns to gravel at the same point today. We never understood why, just assuming someone got crossways with somebody as the project developed. When the county's governing body changed the road's name to County Road 514, it was like stripping the community's most colorful character of all his personality.

A few of us now on our way to old-timer status reject the bland moniker, preferring our memories of the glory days, and we still know it today as Highbanks Road. Despite its modest evolution of name and composition, it's true some things remain the same. When two vehicles meet on Highbanks Road the drivers wave, despite any hard feelings or transgressions short of leaving another man's sister standing at the altar. You wave to your neighbor on Highbanks Road. It's the principal code of the community.

David Watkins' scepter was a .12 gauge semi-automatic Browning, his crown an oil stained International Harvester cap, his chariot a four-wheel-drive Ford F-150 with dirt so thick on the dash you could sprout soybeans. Highbanks Road was a modest country commonwealth, one you'd never even find on a map or amongst the pedigrees of the aristocracy.

He failed and flourished there.

But in his day, my father was its king.

CHAPTER 9

Constant Craving

The things which matter most must never be at the mercy of the things which matter least.

Johann Wolfgang von Goethe

My father's greatest achievement was learning to live large in a small world that revolved mostly around duck hunting, beer drinking, cigarette smoking, loafing, and when absolutely necessary, cotton farming. He was master of all he surveyed, and was as happy as could be, the sovereign lord of a modest and tumultuous life, almost oblivious to anything that wasn't rural Arkansas. He was the big shot of a community that barely had a name.

The forty-year string of rebellion and disdain I held toward him consumed me at times. I made him so irrelevant that I could erase him from all thought for years at a time. But it was a tragic waste of time's precious gift. The shame I projected toward him somehow

made my own inadequacies feel less pronounced. It's what insecure men do. We make the other guy worse than us, and nowhere
is it done better than in the rural South. Southerners invented relative comparison in the accounting of our sins.

Normal conversation about life and everyday things would
have been so refreshing. He never spoke *with* you, but rather, *at*
you and glaring straight through you. Even when he wasn't trying,
his emphatic voice induced a certain intimidating fear. I was never
more envious than times seeing friends have normal, mutually
respectful conversations with their fathers.

What I craved most was a father who liked me, not one who
lorded over me. What he wanted was a well-behaved, dutiful boy
who followed all the rules, stayed quiet, and out of the way. My
father loved boundaries, and he loved enforcing them. Mostly, I
wanted the chance to meet his expectations in exchange for a fleeting moment's acknowledgment. "A job well done, son" every so
often might have made all the difference. He just couldn't do it. If
the sentiment was ever there, and I now believe it was, the words
were never spoken. My rebellion to the rules today, even well into
mid-life, is a product of my father's self-admiration for obedience
toward him — the very same kind he instilled in his many Labra-
dor retrievers who had nothing better to do than fulfill his com-
mands. Sometimes, I envied the dogs. This is the legacy of so many
fathers and sons in 1980s rural America.

But I never lost the deep desire that Daddy would be *for* me.
And, despite his mostly ambivalent attitude, I never stopped trying
to prove a worth that he'd somehow acknowledge — this, even
through the longest periods when I told myself that his approval
mattered not.

The most gut-wrenching thing about disliking my father was the
quiet but constant voice reminding me every day how much I was

supposed to love him and respect him. Because the love instinct is so natural — something in a boy's design always craves his father's pride, and something in a girl's composition wants to see her dad as a proud and valiant protector — the bad feelings get magnified when that's the only choice a father gives.

Loving our dads is a default instinct. It should be so easy. So it's doubly bad carrying enmity toward your father, then resenting that he causes you to feel that way. Guilt poured over the top of hate made me question almost everything about myself. Sometimes, it seemed an emotional paradox that broke my soul completely.

CHAPTER 10

Strongholds: The Farm &
The Father Wound

No one can make you feel inferior without your consent.
Eleanor Roosevelt

On a crisp September day in 1957 the smell of cotton harvest was in the air, but there was surprisingly little to do on his father's small 180-acre farm near Lake City, Arkansas. Seventeen-year-old David Watkins took advantage, deciding he would spend that day with the three things he loved most.

With a nod of self approval to his 1947 Plymouth Coupe that glistened in the gravel driveway, he loaded up a .16 gauge Browning shotgun and headed for the squirrel woods. The young Watkins loved that old car, and he loved being outdoors, but more than anything that year he loved his faithful bird dog, a German short-haired pointer named Tony. He had a way with bird dogs, even at a young age, training them mercilessly with tree branch whippings when they wouldn't obey a command. After so many beatings, they became faithfully his. What he saw as loyalty and love was nothing more than fear of the next beating, but he always loved a dog that would obey his every utterance.

It was one of the best days my young father had enjoyed in a long time, alone in the woods, Tony spot on with every fox-tailed squirrel flying through the pecan tree canopies, and working together they bagged seven nice ones before it was time to return home that day. Tony was muddy all over, and with his beloved Plymouth as clean as could be, Dad saw no harm in putting Tony in the car's trunk for the short sixteen-mile drive home, otherwise the inside would have been a mess. All the drive home he imagined a pot of his mom's famous squirrel and dumplings that would feed the family over a couple of days.

Pulling into the driveway, his mom waited on the front porch for news of the hunt, and dad was so excited about the take he ran straight to her to tell the story. Supper was already on the table and she told him to get cleaned up and he could tell all about it over dinner.

He went to bed that night about as happy as a seventeen-year-old farm boy could be.

But it was a convulsion-like jolt suddenly interrupting that peace the next morning that nearly knocked him out of bed. The sudden realization stole his breath.

Tony!

It couldn't be. There's no way. It's a bad dream, these thoughts racing through his mind as he ran barefoot toward the car still covered with early morning dew. For a moment all he could do was stare at the trunk, key dangling in hand.

Turning the key slowly and raising the lid revealed the nightmare's reality. In the excited moment of arriving home with a limit of squirrels and a story to tell, he'd forgotten all about Tony. Falling to his knees in mourning, my young dad could see his own father watching from the porch. As he approached the scene, my father expected a word of fatherly condolence. Moments after everything seemingly went dark, he found himself face down in the gravel, blood pouring from his lip and a sharp pain running through his jaw, struck moments earlier with the butt end of a Colt revolver. His own father peered down at him with eyes as cold as a north wind, pistol held up against his own chest.

"Pull anything that stupid again and I'll kill you," he said. "Now get that God-damned dog buried."

Some people call it a stronghold.

Paul used the term metaphorically describing some of the especially difficult spiritual battles we encounter. The most unique thing about them, some believe, is that the power to overcome them originates from God alone. Spiritual strongholds come from the deepest wounds that stalk our confidence and crush our character. They are not easily redeemed.

So many strongholds originate in the relationships where we have the most love. And the most vulnerability.

Sherman "Short" Watkins was my grandfather. He was both a simple and complicated man, also a farmer. He wanted his three meals a day, with meat, two sides, and light bread, served at precisely the same time with a pitcher of ice water within arm's reach, just to his right. Despite the convenient proximity, my grandmother always poured it for him. He watched St. Louis Cardinals baseball religiously from a vinyl rocker-recliner that you didn't dare sit in yourself, and he rolled his own Prince Albert cigarettes while drinking steaming hot coffee, even if it was a hundred degrees outside. He enjoyed the methodical ritual of rolling his cigarettes so much, it could be hypnotic as you watched. Each night, he read the local paper in bed, grandma next to him clad in a cotton house coat and hair net.

And for a man of his generation, he was sharply passive-aggressive, if not downright mean in situations where he felt threatened by the success of anyone subordinate, especially his only son. These are the things I most vividly remember about the grandfather on my father's side, the man I called Papa, along with a story my mother shared a decade after my own father's passing.

In 1964, my father believed he had it all. A job away from the farm, his prized 1958 Ford Fairlane, and he was dating one of the most eligible women in Craighead County. He had no intent for anything to change. But after a yearlong courtship, my mom gave him an ultimatum that they be married or go their separate ways. There was a shotgun wedding the very next day.

It caught my father off guard in more ways than one, including financially. He'd somehow found the courage to ask his own father for a loan of forty dollars for the Mountain View, Arkansas honeymoon, and may have been even more surprised when his father granted the loan. As the weeks passed, my dad either forgot about the loan, or assumed it a gift. The latter was a poor assumption.

Only two weeks later, my grandfather initiated a private moment with my mom and asked that she repay the forty dollars her new husband had failed to repay. It was all news to her, and the first indication of a foreign family dynamic she'd live with another forty years.

There is something in every man's DNA that wants to make his father proud. It's true in the best, and in the worst of father-son relationships. Maybe God made it that way to help us understand our feelings toward Him. St. Augustine knew this sixteen hundred years ago. "Thou has formed us for thyself and our hearts are restless until they find rest in thee."

Even today, seven years since my father's death, I find myself working feverishly to fill a void I never even knew existed. Whether you're six or sixty, all the rebellion in the world will never extinguish the flame a son has to make his father proud.

My grandparents, Short and Burty Watkins as they were known, lived thirty miles away in an even more rural and secluded Arkansas area than we did. Through the first ten years of my parents' marriage, there was at least a monthly visit — they to our place, or we to theirs. They were just beyond subsistence farmers, raising a small acreage of cotton, soybeans, and cantaloupes, and they frequently preserved pork and beef in an old smokehouse — enough to fill their bellies through the long winters. They seemed entirely happy living this way.

Together, they shared three daughters and a son. The more time passed, the more it seemed the family drew closer even as the daughters married and had their own families. Long weekend visits and overnights to the old home place were common. My dad was the exception, in fact the opposite. The more time passed, the more he became distant from the family, especially staying clear of his father. He almost never spoke of the man who refused to offer even an occasional kind or encouraging word.

The year I was eight years old, Grandma and Papa came for a Sunday visit in the late summer season. Dad had just advanced in stature from small farmer to medium-sized farmer with additional acreage and new equipment, and he'd purchased a used International Harvester tractor giving him the capacity to move from four-row to six-row capacity. The tractor had several hundred hours service, but was newly painted and its acquisition was a proud moment for my dad. In just four years, and still a young man at age thirty-one, he'd exceeded his own father's agricultural success.

After a Sunday meal (mom always felt a certain expectation for putting home-cooked food on the table when they visited) and not long after Papa labeled my mom's lemon meringue pie topping "calf slobber," Daddy invited Papa for a stroll to the tractor shed to see the new equipment.

"What do you think?" he asked, looking for approval. I trailed along behind at a distance.

"Well, I guess you think you're a big shot now," his reply. "I don't know why anyone needs something like that." He spoke the words just low enough that it sounded like a quiet thought, yet loud enough they were heard.

Moments like these between fathers and sons can change the course of a relationship forever.

There was a louder and more heated exchange as they got closer to the driveway. It seemed suddenly that years of animosity poured out. I watched as my grandfather told my father what a sorry son-of-a-bitch he was. Hate radiated from his eyes. I could see my father restraining his own reaction to keep it from becoming a physical encounter. It ended with my grandmother obeying a command to get in the truck, and my father yelling at his father to never come back. It wasn't the first such exchange. Years later, in an unusually candid moment, my father shared with me through tears the story about the pistol whipping and Tony. He could never forget the image of a gun held above him at his own father's hand.

A year of silence between them followed without a real apology or reconciliation. They began speaking again at an extended family gathering in Kansas, but their disdain for each other never diminished.

My grandfather died four years later from what we now believe was a prescription drug opioid addiction. Had the information available today been available back then, the signs would have been obvious. I've never seen a man weep as my father did standing at that casket. It was hard to tell whether he was sad about the loss, or the relationship that never really was.

Years later, it was easy understanding the truth of it all — my grandfather was to his son, the very same thing my father was to me. But my dad wasn't an innately mean man, and much of who he was resulted from his struggle with his own self-worth. How is a grown man supposed to feel when his father points a pistol at him?

TURN ROW

My father was far more in control of himself with me than his father was with him. There was never a time when I was scared for my life, but scared many times, nonetheless. It wasn't a spanking you got for discipline. It was a whipping. My last one might not have been so bad had he not exercised the discipline in anger.

For years we kept a couple of pet mallard ducks in a small raised pen. Why, I never knew, for they brought no real pleasure to anyone and were contained completely outside their natural element, but we did, and they were my responsibility. Feeding the ducks with water and ground corn was a daily chore that I often turned to every other day or more. Skipping days was lazy at best, and better described as just plain cruel.

The freezing-cold winter of 1976 was hard on everyone, including farm animals. I'd skipped a day or two on the feedings when my father caught me in a lie after finding both ducks frozen solid in the pen, their lack of warmth likely not helped from a lack of food. He forced me to stand at the pen staring at the frozen carcasses for ten minutes, the shame before the pain.

Watching him walk across the yard to strip a one-inch limb from a poplar tree, I knew what was coming. He was as angry as I'd ever seen. Grabbing me by the left arm he commanded me to bend over. The first strike to my backside felt like it brought blood. This wasn't going to be a spanking. It was a whipping. He must have lashed me a dozen times until I thought I'd pass out. As I walked away in silence, he called me back, grabbed me, and lashed out another six times. This time, I crumbled to the ground. I came to thirty minutes later and went to bed with no supper. I heard him tell mom the next morning that he'd let himself get of control because he was angry. It was the last physical punishment he ever inflicted.

CHAPTER 11

Just Enough Jesus To Be Miserable

*I think it is safe to say that while the South is hardly
Christ-centered, it is most certainly Christ-haunted.*

Flannery O'Connor

He always told it as a joke and laughed harder than anybody in
the room. But I sometimes wonder if my father's story about his
first day in the Army National Guard was secretly more hurtful
than humorous.

In his later years, Dad was proud that he'd served a brief stint
in the military. One day, I noticed he'd framed and displayed his
honorable discharge in the shop where he spent most of his day
time. He mostly loved talking about how much he hated the experience, and poked some real self-deprecating fun at himself in the
story that transpired almost immediately after he stepped off a bus
in Fort Polk, Louisiana.

It's a story reminiscent of the words actor George C. Scott recited in the 1970 movie *Patton* when he played the famous lead role. It was a fiery speech where the legendary figure encouraged his troops to battle. "And one day as you're sitting at your fireside with your grandson on your knee and he asks, 'Grandfather, what did you do in the great war?' at least you won't have to say, 'Well, I shoveled shit in Louisiana.'"

Without fanfare or military regalia, this is precisely what my father did.

He shoveled excrement in the steaming hot Louisiana bayou.

Fort Polk is no garden spot. It may actually be the most ideal place on the planet for shoveling human poop.

In 1962, Fort Polk was converted to an advanced infantry training center. A portion of the base is filled with dense, jungle-like vegetation. This, along with Louisiana's heat, humidity, and precipitation, helped commanders acclimatize new infantry soldiers in preparation for Vietnam combat. For the next twelve years, more soldiers were shipped to Vietnam from Fort Polk than from any other American training base. In 1969, my father took a chance that his volunteer service in the Guard might lessen his chances of getting shipped overseas. He was right, but it was a risk.

After an eight-hour bus ride from Jonesboro, Arkansas, buck private David Watkins was boots on the ground for basic training. It was a reality check moment for all the recruits, many of whom had never been beyond the Arkansas state line. They had no idea how radically and completely their lives would change in the next twenty minutes.

Their first bumbling march in the Louisiana heat was toward a massive barracks for supply distribution. They joined the back of a long, winding line making its way through various stations. Health and hygiene stations first, where each received his first GI "haircut" in twenty seconds flat, then on to immunizations, shots in both arms simultaneously with something that looked like advanced weaponry designed to kill aliens. They called it a military vaccine jet gun.

Slowly, but efficiently, troops moved to basic clothing and supplies, where unforgiving enlisted men loaded each recruit down. Standard latrine kit. Boots. GI socks. Army green cap. And then my father came to the underwear station.

Enlisted men only six weeks senior to the recruits were barking orders so fast and loud it was chaotic and confusing. The frenzy was by design, and every once in a while they led gullible guys like Bay, Arkansas native David Watkins right into their trap.

In the midst of the turmoil, Dad got in a hurry and tried on his boxers backwards, fly wide open on the back side. And just when he thought he'd escaped any observation.

"Hold it right there, son!" an authoritative voice from a few feet away commanded.

A drill sergeant immediately jumped up on a table, blew a whistle, and stopped all the activity. Hundreds of men came to a silent standstill. The drill sergeant's hands were raised high in the air to garner maximum dramatic attention. In the now silent barracks, he echoed an announcement.

"What's your name, soldier?" the man asked looking down on my ill-at-ease father.

"David Watkins."

"David Watkins, what, son?" the screaming got louder.

"David Watkins, drill sergeant!"

"Well, at least you know your own name," the sergeant said, turning full circle on the table for a group announcement.

"Men, meet David Watkins, who as you can see, prefers to wear his underwear backwards, fly in the back, an automatic shit hole, I presume. I do believe this is the dumbest son-of-a-bitch ever to come through Fort Polk, Louisiana! I just wanted you to meet him. Carry on!"

The whole place erupted, every single laugh directed at Dad.

He always told that story with great enthusiasm and lots of belly laughing. But I always thought about how such moments can wound a young man forever.

Never did I think more about my father's hidden insecurities than in church. For most of his seventy-three years he carried a deep sense of unworthiness, and a picture of a God who lorded over a man who would never measure up. It didn't take an advanced psychology degree to see this. His body language in certain environments. The way he would avoid certain topics. The attitude he held toward many who'd taken time for a greater understanding about deeper things. The mean streak in him was a product of all the things he didn't know, and the frightened expectation he had about them all. He imagined a fearful day of accountability with a disappointed God, and one where his side of the scale didn't stand a chance.

The church was always a part of our lives — but it was as much a family tradition and weekly ritual as some personal interaction with a divine power.

My dad knew just enough about Jesus to be miserable.

Real, genuine understanding — the kind that anchors us in a fixed belief and serves as a reliable point of moral reference — is an experience so personal it's not a path down which anyone else can lead us. There's a hollow sense that comes with just about any notion prompted by persuasion. And there's an abyss between the realms of persuaded and convinced. Believing is your responsibility, a product of your own authentic quest for truth.

The God of my youth was one in whom I believed through the persuasion of circumstances, and surroundings, and pretty much because of what other people said. Everything about growing up in the Highbanks Community north of Monette, Arkansas pointed to a life where we went to church and believed in God, not uncommonly in that misconceived order. It took another thirty years finding the joy of convinced certainty that comes from a pursuit absent persuasion, and more about the thrill of relationship and quest.

But from birth to adolescence and into young adulthood, I believed. That's just what we did. We grew cotton, loved our high school basketball, hunted ducks, and we believed in God.

A dozen or more families that went back four generations on the church roll gathered each Sunday at Macey United Methodist Church a quarter mile north of Highbanks Road. It was a simple shotgun style church constructed with blonde cinder block style brick with cotton farms to the south and west. Bobby Joe Pitts' farm shop was across the gravel road north, International Harvester tractors, planters, and cultivators plainly in sight. There was no asphalt lot divided into neat parking spaces, just a patch of gravel here and there. Most men with four-wheel drive pickup trucks parked on weedy grass consumed with dandelions and ugly clumps of crab grass. An old massive and rusting propane tank stood conspicuously amongst it all.

There was a community call to worship each Sunday morning at nine when Curly Hout opened the building and rang the big bell nine times signaling an hour to Sunday school. The cast-bronze bell just underneath the white spiraled steeple resounded a dozen miles or more across the Arkansas Delta flatlands on a quiet Sunday morning, shooing blackbirds from their peaceful home the other six days of the week. Our family always stopped everything, listening and counting along as if Curly might miss a lick. It was a thrill after church each week when the men let me pull the thick, knotted bell rope signaling the end of worship. My small frame came right off the ground against the rope's tension and the bell's heavy weight. Tinkie Wimberley held me up shoulder high oftentimes so I could get enough leverage to make at least one good clang. "There you go, Stevie," Tinkie would say, patting me on the back, and I'd giggle with delight.

Rumors circulated for years through the mid-seventies that the state's Methodist church bureaucracy wanted the old country church closed and consolidated with the "city church" five miles south in Monette. Paid for in full decades earlier through the private gifts from dozens of community families, distant administrators in the state church bureaucracy preferred the church razed than sold outright to another denomination. It wouldn't be right having those charismatic people in our church even if we no longer had a use for it, they reasoned.

On a spring day in 1973, the small congregation gathered a final time and voted they would comply with the orders. My mother and grandmother sobbed walking out the door, believing it created a hole in the rural community's heart that would never be filled. Never again would the community church pastor be invited for Sunday dinner. Never again would Millie Wimberley allow me back into the community room to help break crackers and pour grape juice for communion. I wondered for a moment if the new church would have as good a place for hunting Easter eggs as we'd always enjoyed there. The sadness about losing the church was like a fog over the community for years.

Volunteers finally demolished the building and the rubble remained strewn about the property another five years. The eyesore was a constant reminder of what made locals feel as though their church had pushed them around and stolen a holy identity.

Only seven years old when we moved to the big church inside the city limits, I sensed resentment from the country church people who'd been forced to move into the new congregation now some seventy to eighty strong. I remember thinking how odd it was feeling like a stranger in the place they called God's house. It was the first *we vs. them* environment I remember, and it took years healing that community wound.

Of children in a marriage where the father doesn't attend church, only one in fifty becomes a frequent and active church member in adulthood. Another survey shows that when a family's father becomes the first parent declaring himself a Christ follower, children will follow at a rate of 93 percent, as opposed to a 17 percent probability of the children following when a mother is first to declare her faith.

According to LifeWay Research Group, Father's Day is the holiday with the single lowest average church attendance — statistically lower than Labor Day, Memorial Day and even the Fourth of July. Interesting, when you consider that Mother's Day, has the third highest church service attendance, after Easter and Christmas.

Much of this, I suppose, makes me an anomaly.

At home, we never had any real conversation about the reasons for going to church each Sunday. Like the weekly trip to Flannigan's Grocery Store, it was just something we did without discussion or thought. A dusty copy of The Living Bible stayed visible on a small bookshelf in our home, but I never remember talking about God or seeing Mom or Dad read that Bible. We certainly never talked about what was in it. We went to church and believed in what happened there, but it was all a private and personal experience not really up for discussion. Mom and I were almost always there, back row, right corner, while Dad attended every Easter, and as the mood struck him.

Though it was an open invitation to all, never once did I see my father take communion. As the preacher called us to the kneeling altar near the platform, he always stepped aside allowing others to go forward and he'd stand in the back corner, hands clasped uncomfortably behind his back, until we returned to the pew. An awkward observer. Though we never really discussed it, my young spirit sensed that Dad just didn't feel worthy participating in the sacrament. Even as a child it was hard knowing he felt that way, and I would spend all day wondering what troubled him so. It didn't seem right that unworthiness and shame would have a place in church, I remember thinking, and I'm not sure a single person ever discussed with him why he felt so trapped in consuming guilt.

We all have our demons.

Methodist church philosophy dictated that it was best a preacher not stay in one place too long. Just about the time they'd begin making a community fingerprint, a formal letter from the bishop arrived with marching orders that it was on to the next town. A three-year tenure was about average, and small towns like ours usually ended up with old men near retirement, or those who were just downright strange like Brother Buford Bell, a large-lipped rotund man who wore suits three sizes too small, and was unable to turn his neck. Put him in one of those tight suits and have something abrupt happen and all he could do was hop around to get a glimpse. Each Sunday he'd go to the shelf and dust off an old sermon from fifteen years ago. The congregation got three points in monotone voice for twenty minutes and there was usually some metaphor about a flower in bloom. There's a good chance I would have pursued a career in the ministry myself if almost every preacher that came along hadn't seemed so completely miserable.

Through the late seventies and eighties, the church highlight for me was watching Russell Strickland sing the bass line to *He Arose* each Easter. His voice also dominated the Doxology just following the giving of tithes and offerings every Sunday. It was fun watching Russell reach for a really low note. His eyes turned downward slightly and his head shook just a bit.

When a dashing young fellow by the name of Rev. David Bentley sauntered into town one spring day, everyone believed someone in the church assignment hierarchy made a grievous mistake. Bentley was edgy before edgy was even a thing, and he was like nothing we'd seen before. He had young children, a wife who was engaged in ministry, and personality. Boy, did David

Bentley have personality. He was Don Quixote in a beat-up Chevy station wagon, with the radio dial likely tuned to Rock 103, the Memphis station popular among the high schoolers.

Bentley's sermons were fresh, his delivery bold and spirited, and they were about real life. *So this is what church is like*, I remember thinking. He didn't have to convince you of anything — even I recognized his teaching applications. He couldn't have been more than a few months into his tenure when one day he really got our attention.

Altar call after altar call, invitation after invitation, with a congregation as engaged as knots on logs, and not so much as a single act of repentance or heart for Christ, Bentley one day had enough. He stopped the organist mid-melody, and for another ten minutes preached like no one in that little small-town church had ever seen — I'd never seen hell-fire and brimstone, but was pretty sure that was it — and scolded the church family like a coach's team down twenty at halftime. Every single member went forward and rededicated their life to Jesus. The next week, everyone just sat there like always, but at least Bentley made his point. He never went on a tirade like that again.

Early in my seventh-grade year, Rev. Bentley gathered a small group of six young people and passed out a magazine-like document headlined *Your Confirmation*. He said that he and his wife would like to take us on a long weekend to the lake because it was time for that Methodist milestone. I didn't know what confirmation meant then, and am still not quite clear what it means today, but Missy Cranford was going along and I had a junior high crush on her, so confirmation sounded fine. At the weekend retreat, we swam, went water skiing, cooked some nice meals, and read through a booklet that told us we were ready for the responsibilities of adult Christianity. Two weeks later we stood at the altar, got sprinkled from an ornate can, and I was confirmed, whatever that meant. And I suppose it stuck. A few years later, witnessing my first Baptist baptism with full immersion, I assumed confirmation had been the equivalent, absent the hands held high and seemingly impromptu and on-cue collective voices singing the chorus of *To God Be the Glory*. Even as a child I loved visiting the Baptist Church. The worship seemed deeper somehow. More like what God would want. The best-looking girls went there, too.

Then one day our little town had a crazy progressive idea. Church leaders from the Baptists, Assembly of God, and Methodists got together, deciding they'd hold a joint Sunday night service every four months or so, and that we'd focus mostly on singing and preaching. The Church of Christ opted out because there would be musical instruments on site, and apparently God viewed musical instruments as sinful. The services were a big success, and I always thought we Methodists got the best end of the deal. When the Baptists hosted, we got to go to their big church, and when the Assembly of God hosted, they took music and charismatic environments to levels we'd never seen. It was the first time I'd ever watched people speak in tongues and run around jumping and hollering in a church building for no apparent reason. But boy, was it invigorating!

Twenty years later there was an agreement for the Church of Christ to join in. Everything went fine until it came their time to host, and the other three churches got a memo to leave their instruments and taped music behind. And oh, add this one to the new rules and regulations — no public speaking roles for any of the ladies. Thus, it all ended about as quickly as it began.

As quickly as David Bentley came, he went, and the bureaucracy moved him on to bigger and better things. Bentley was a rising star in the Arkansas Methodist Church, and shone too brightly for Monette, Arkansas.

The subsequent decision to send Rev. Jack Regal set us back a decade and nearly crushed my new-found pursuit of a God who, at around seventeen, I could actually perceive as working in my life.

Regal was bald, overweight, had terrible teeth, and he stank a little. His sermons were flat, and he bored church members, but most people in the outside community generally liked him and enjoyed his gregarious nature — perhaps more of his need for approval. He drove a beat-up Buick long as a boat, drank coffee with the locals, and rarely missed a high school basketball game.

I was friendly with Regal, but never engaged with him as much as he'd have liked. Even as a young teen, perceptions made me uncomfortable around him.

One day during basketball practice on the far end of the gym floor I noticed Regal standing in the entry way leading from the lobby toward the bleachers. He was near the water fountain, just where I was headed.

After a long drink, Regal grabbed my shoulder as if desperate for attention and a laugh. Then he shared a joke apparently believing it was the funniest thing he'd ever told, and he guffawed with that stinking breath.

For a split second things went black. It was some of the filthiest language I'd heard then, or to this day. Suddenly, the spiritual leader of my church felt like a dirty old man capable of anything. No moment ever felt more wrong.

Breaking his grip on my shoulder, I ran away not looking back, and never had the courage to speak to him again. The unspoken tension between us remained through the next two years of his term and put a dent in my spiritual growth for years.

Flipping through the newspaper pages one day thirty years later I came across his obituary.

Other than an eyes-closed cringe, there no was emotion. Just hurt and disappointment.

TURN ROW

In his book, *To the Field of Stars*, Father Kevin Codd gives an interesting explanation for why so many people in the modern era are drawn to the idea of pilgrimage. It was widely believed in medieval times that when a pilgrimage concluded, especially if you were in a village where a saint worked, or where the bones of that saint were interred, you were in a "thin realm," a place closer to heaven than anywhere else you could be on earth.

It poses a question I pondered frequently as a child. *Where does God live?* My young mind needed God to *be* somewhere. Omniscience, omnipotence, and omnipresence aren't easy concepts for a kid.

Just above and behind our choir loft in the Monette First United Methodist Church was a long pair of red velvet-like drapes, the kind you might normally see covering a baptistry, and a big wooden cross that seemed to hang in thin air. Every time the preacher talked about the blood of Jesus I stared at those crimson curtains.

What lie behind them was always a mystery as no kid ever had the courage to look. I decided God's spirit lived behind those curtains. I needed to know God was somewhere, and behind the veil, He was close enough, and just far enough away.

CHAPTER 12

Barber Shops

Sometimes you want to go where everybody knows your name ...
    Lyrics to the theme song from the television show Cheers

There are lots of places you can get a haircut. David Watkins went to the barber shop. That's just the kind of man he was.

Every small town still had one in the eighties, and they were easy to find. Outside you'd see it. A revolving pole with red, white, and blue stripes, and a silver cap at top and bottom. It is an ancient symbol of the generations that might as well say *men only*. Barber shops were rejecting political correctness before rejecting political correctness was cool.

It would make the Top 3 list of loafing centers in any small town, but the banter in a barbershop takes loafing and tall tales to DEFCON Level 2. For people like my dad who had no interest in far-fetched ideas like personal growth or civic responsibility, the barber shop was the ultimate safe place. Even in an age when the next generation of young men was already migrating to the less manly salon, or some family hair care center void of all character, the barber shop was a monthly bright spot for some, a higher frequency for many who just liked being there. Avoiding it altogether, dad's hair must have grown six inches that summer Elmer Duncan beat him black and blue for his trouble.

There is no great philosophical lesson, nor will you hear much about things like caramel lattes or shoulder bags for men in barber shops across the South. More likely, there will be a funny story featuring one of the Baptist deacons getting caught with the post mistress on a turn row off Highbanks Road last Saturday night. Or someone might pass around a blurry, dog-eared Polaroid of a twelve-point buck he got down in the bottoms when that cold front moved through last week. Both stories will grow exponentially more dramatic through the community from there. In a few days, the deacon will have two black eyes, and that buck swam the river channel before he gave out and died.

The actual goal of any barbershop visit is leaving clean and refreshed, ready to take on the world. Mostly after a haircut at Roger's Barber Shop you left smelling more like one of Roger Darmer's old cigars. The fat stogies were always tucked away in the right corner of Roger's mouth while he worked, and you'd have to brush the ashes off your shoulders when you left.

One thing making it so memorable is the barber shop's full sensory experience.

It begins with your nose the moment you walk through the door. Imagine an invisible swirling diffusion of talcum powder, shaving cream, cigar smoke, and hard liquor inevitably on the

alcoholic barber's breath. He always worked in one of two conditions — drunk or hung over. Roger slurred his speech, and I never
knew if it was a natural slur or the effects from the fifth of Old
Charter he kept on a corner shelf just around the door leading to
the storage room. Though he couldn't enunciate so well, you just
hoped Roger could hear what you needed. Not that it mattered
so much. There were two standard offerings at Roger's — a trim
or a cut. Either meant whatever Roger felt like doing at the time.
That was just his personality. In a fashion era when it was popular
for men to wear personalized belts with their name imprinted on
the back center, Roger's belt actually read, *BELT*.

A broad mirror mounted on the wall behind the two barber
chairs enhanced the poor lighting and drew even greater attention to one or more fluorescent light bulbs on the blink. Your
boots clapped on the twenty-year-old outdated vinyl floor as you
made your way to one of the Naugahyde chairs, some splitting and
repaired with duct or electrical tape. On the far wall just below the
Pepsi clock sat a platform-elevated shoe shine stand that looked
like a king's throne. In all the years at Roger's, I never witnessed
a single shine, though it was fun sitting in the big chair awaiting
your turn in the barber chair. There were no numbers or spread-
sheets. You knew it was your turn when all the men who were in
the shop when you came in were no longer there.

There were no fashion or style magazines lying around, but lots
of old copies of *Popular Mechanics*, *Progressive Farmer*, and *MAD
Magazine*. A big Snap-On Tool poster above the mirror featured
a barely clothed model wearing bright, red lipstick and stretched
across a hot-rod car hood. It was strictly about the ratchet and
socket set almost outside the frame. One framed sign on Roger's
counter near the money drawer always set the customer-friendly
tone: *I can only please one person a day. Today is not your day, and
tomorrow ain't looking too good, either.*

The mood lightened a bit any time a child came in for his first haircut, which was always a big deal. Roger had a booster seat for young boys that set them up high, and the old-timers always encouraged the nervous youngsters as Roger clipped away. You always hoped it was one of his hungover days, and that he didn't bring blood to an ear. It happened, traumatizing more than one kid in town. Blood or no blood, you got a piece of bubble gum when the ordeal was over, and so you eternally forgave Roger the laceration.

He may not have been the most talented barber on earth, but Roger Darmer gave a heck of a straight-razor touch-up, and aside from the good company it was the best thing about the barber shop experience. When the clipping and trimming was complete, Roger placed a hot towel around your neck and left it there a minute or two. Meanwhile, he'd take a straight razor across a long, leather strop and give it a clean edge with quick back and forth motions. Just before he removed the towel you'd hear the mechanical noise of a hot lather machine as he cupped his left hand with enough foam to spread around your neckline and above the ears. Methodically, he'd scrape away the rough edges leaving the finest, most perfect line a barber can cut. Just as he'd finish, he would use his fingertips massaging around your ears and the back of your neck for a minute or two and finish wiping away the remaining lather with a fresh hot towel. You never wanted that last part of a haircut to end.

A little talcum powder on a soft brush whisked around your neckline and forehead finished off the experience, except for Roger's signature sign-off line as he whirled the chair around so you were looking at yourself dead straight in the mirror.

"Ain't that pretty?" he'd ask every single time. "You're pretty again."

If David Watkins had been a barber, he'd have been a lot like Roger Darmer.

CHAPTER 13

Fencerows

*We tend to think of landscapes as affecting us most strongly
when we are in them or on them, when they offer us the
primary sensations of touch and sight. But there are also
the landscapes we bear with us in absentia, those places
that live on in memory long after they have withdrawn in
actuality, and such places - retreated to most often when we
are most remote from them - are among the most important landscapes we possess.*

Robert Macfarlane

On the snowy days when we'd load up the shotguns and take the
four-wheel drive pickup across the countryside and up and down
every fencerow, I didn't mind the cigarette smoke or dad's occasional beer. Chasing rabbits and quail, or anything else that left

tracks was an adventure that made you oblivious to everything except the adrenaline of the hunt.

But at our own hand, and in the name of progress, fencerows have practically vanished from the rural landscape. It was like stripping the life-giving blood vessels from inside a living being. No longer do the fencerows of rural America paint the countryside with character and color that defined a bucolic way of life.

They were far more than just lines of demarcation between forty-acre fields.

During the seventies and early eighties, it seemed to most of us the fencerows were landmarks as fixed as the country roads themselves — something that always had been, and would be into the future. Neither was actually true.

Initiated by the Roosevelt administration in 1934 in a project known as The Great Plains Shelterbelt, fencerows were created as windbreaks and erosion control in response to the windstorms of the Dust Bowl. By 1942, some 220 million trees were planted, stretching for 18,600 miles. The very first tree in the program was an Austrian pine planted near Willow, Oklahoma in 1935.

The fencerows didn't eliminate wind erosion, but they helped, and as a perk brought an unanticipated dimension to the countryside, infusing it with life. As the trees grew and the fencerow strips became thicker with ground cover, briar thickets, and vines, a whole new economy enveloped rural America. Across the Delta, fencerows became abundant with wildlife like squirrel, opossum, raccoon, a dozen bird varieties including game birds like quail and pheasant, and cold-blooded reptiles. The fencerow habitat on our farms was the perfect location for several fox dens over the years. And in exchange for a few jars of raw honey each year, farmers gave free passage to the many beekeepers who placed their hives in the fencerows. Wild honeysuckle and soybean blooms were abundant pollen sources for hundreds of fencerow hives.

After duck season and during the heavy snows, there was nothing the sportsmen enjoyed more than taking their bird dogs out to run the fencerows for quail. A well-trained bird dog that works and points a covey of quail is one of nature's most beautiful sights. For many years early each fall, the Arkansas Game & Fish Commission sponsored a fish fry at the local American Legion where you could buy quail by the dozen and release them into the fence row habitat. All the young boys got to watch an educational film — usually a different film each year, executed with the same routine — while the men drank beer out back. It seemed the wildlife officers spent forever spooling the old reel to reel projector with film that broke at least two or three times during the show. Occasionally, the film would get stuck too close to the bulb creating an ominous image akin to nuclear meltdown. But it was enduring one of those ancient films where I first learned about living in a place so important to wildlife that it even had a really cool name — the Mississippi River Flyway. Made you feel kind of proud — *we actually were from somewhere.*

Faced with tough financial decisions after the 1980 drought, the dwindling number of farmers with enough remaining resources to play the long game invested heavily in irrigation which required precision-leveled land. Not a square inch is spared in the leveling process. Within three years the fencerows, and all they provided, disappeared from the landscape. Today, the most productive farmland in the world is barren and without character in the off season. It all looks the same.

It was only about six years before we destroyed the fencerows that a few small government entities actually encouraged us to preserve them.

The U.S. Soil Conservation Service offered farmers free loblolly pines in the spring of 1975. The seedlings, no more than eight inches in height, were proven effective wind breaks, they grew fast, and brought a new, evergreen dimension to the landscape. The free incentive actually carried a stiff on-your-honor price — your signed pledge to plant every single one for the benefit of the agricultural community. Quantities began at a thousand.

During most of March 1975, armed with two flat shovels and a tow sack each, Dad and I planted a thousand trees. All up and down Highbanks Road and across the Macey community, wherever there existed a square foot of vacant ground, a pine tree was sown. Insert shovel into the ground, spread it apart a bit, insert seedling, push the ground back together. That's about all there was to it. Springtime rains and sunshine did the rest.

Just about the time we'd planted half the countryside and only a few dozen seedlings remained, Mom and Dad jointly decided we'd tear out an old dying fencerow on the eastern side of our home property and replant it with the fast growing pines. For Dad, it was a windbreak to his over-sized vegetable garden. For Mom, an impenetrable shield from an overly-curious neighbor with a party line just across the north forty.

After tearing the old fencerow out, we had piles of scrub brush, tree limbs, and old stumps piled high, fuel for the kind of fire that will burn for days if you kept it properly "chunked." That first night I noticed Dad wasn't in his standard eight o'clock prone position on the couch. Mom said he was outside with the fire.

I walked out and found him lying on the ground, head propped against a log, and a small twig in his mouth. It was one of the most uncharacteristic scenes I ever recall. Peaceful, relaxed, enjoying the warmth of a fire on a cool spring evening.

"Sit out here with me a while," he said, in an almost foreign, brotherly tone.

I pulled up a log and for the next several hours we enjoyed one of the best conversations I remember. Lying back, we stared heavenward in amazement as the occasional meteor streaked in, then out of the atmosphere. We reflected on the experience of planting a thousand trees together, and laughed at how hard it had been. We wondered how the countryside might change because of our efforts. For those few hours, it was almost as if we were equal.

In the several weeks we spent together planting those trees, I don't recall my father speaking a single harsh word about anyone, or anything.

There was so much hope laced into those unanticipated times of peace.

CHAPTER 14

The Art Of Loafing In A Parts Store

It is impossible to enjoy idling thoroughly unless one has plenty of work to do.

Jerome K. Jerome

When you think on it, it's amazing just how much of nothing can go on in a little town. In the seventies and eighties, Monette, Arkansas had at least a half dozen places dedicated to doing nothing. If you wished to laggard about and pick up on the latest second-hand hearsay, there was a group and a place just for you.

Claud Earl Barnett's parts store was headquarters for some of the older, more refined, and even religious town loafers. It was an exclusive club, as much because of confined quarters as anything, and the store was configured so patrons could park around back. Those who took a view from main street were none the wiser who was inside.

Farmers like Dad had two primary loafing hot spots. The offices at Keich-Shauver Gin were appointed with fifteen wooden chairs around the periphery where some of the more legitimate loafing took place and the topics focused mostly on farming. Gin manager Raymond Miller was one of the smartest men in town, the kind of man a kid could listen to forever. Raymond fascinated me with stories on things he'd read about — space exploration, weather, endangered species lists. It seemed he was one of the few men actually interested in things that happened outside the city limits. His voice carried a natural authority.

Not a hundred yards south at Ball-Hout Implement, the local dealer for International Harvester, was where the real cutups loafed and the tallest tales got told. Of course, it was David Watkins' go-to place of belonging. Oftentimes, I thought, the center of his world.

Loafing hours started at 6 A M and ended at 5 each afternoon. Ball-Hout, known to locals as the International (Harvester) Place, was the only location in town with a room dedicated entirely to hosting town loafers. It was a rectangular room with two extra-long couches and a couple of vinyl cushion chairs. There was an industrial-sized coffee pot that parts manager Doyle "One-Eye" Yates freshened on the hour. All this across from the long parts counter and a small room where you could buy Nocona boots and toy tractors. The store and its loafing customers were so amalgamated, there was a huge framed art piece above the parts counter featuring a Western bar scene with dozens of characters, each named for a store employee or a special customer. I spent hours admiring the piece in the near eighteen years I accompanied my dad there. It hung until the store closed forty years later.

In many ways, loafing with Dad at the International Place taught me a lot about what it meant to be a man. One day you'd hear stories of uncommon valor from some of World War II, Korea and Vietnam's bravest veterans like J.L. Kimbrell or Tinkie Wimberley. The next, a rambling tale from some of town's most lovable drunks. It was in the International Place where I learned that in casual settings a man can cross his legs one of two ways — with one leg perpendicular straight across the other, or hanging down across the other, dangling, in a more feminine sort of way. Some of the toughest men in town went with the feminine style, and by four years old I was replicating their behavior — a young boy's admiration for some of America's finest. A little of each lives on in every child who ever loafed there with his dad.

Those in a certain club loafed at the emergency medical ambulance service in back of City Hall. It was mostly about card playing there, a game called pitch. Charles Kelley, our town's only garbage man — beloved for his colorful style of umpiring softball games, and for his occasional public performances imitating Elvis Presley — would frequently slip away from work to play pitch, despite the unease and constant awareness that the mayor's office was just two doors down the hall.

There was even a dedicated spot between two old elm trees on Main Street next to Flannigan's General Store where the oldest men sat on wooden benches, recalled their glory days, and enjoyed the occasional drink of cold, clean water from a hand-pumped well. Young folk named it for a part of the old men's anatomy, and make-believe stories of their waning sexual vitality.

It's true, we all need to belong somewhere, and everyone needs a tribe. And it's all the more fun when the members poke fun at themselves.

But we also have a responsibility to ourselves that community not just be found in the shallow places. Community should be comfortable, enjoyable, a place of acceptance where no judgment gets passed. Community should also go deep. It should challenge us, hold us accountable, inspire us to grow — a place where we can look around and model the servant-leadership that Jesus exhibited.

Dr. Robert Lewis teaches in his curriculum, *The Quest for Authentic Manhood,* that most men are just standing in a line waiting for someone to come to them, outstretch a hand, and offer friendship. Every man, Lewis says, needs a cheerleader.

It was easy for Dad to hang out at the International Place or the gin. Nothing really challenged anything about him in those places. He avoided gatherings like the United Methodist men's groups, the VFW, or the masonic lodge, all those places where mentors and cheerleaders were in strong supply.

Dad was always one of those guys standing in the line with everybody else. He just never could muster up the courage to stretch out a hand to a man he admired and ask, *Will you be my friend?*

It was his lack of deep connections that would one day weigh heavy on my own sense of responsibility and create a serious role reversal in our relationship.

TURN ROW

Is there a difference in loafing and piddling?

In a column for *Southern Living Magazine,* Pulitzer Prize-winning journalist Rick Bragg makes the distinction.

While loafing is more of a social affair absent of intent or outcome, piddling may have goals and may be pursued as a solo activity. Bragg writes:

"It is hard to explain to begin with, because piddling is neither one thing or another, but something in between. It is not rest, not something that can be done with your feet on an ottoman or as you recline in a Posturepedic. But then neither is it work, something that one toils at, sweats at, something one needs a break from, for lunch, coffee. It is certainly not something for which one should ever be paid, and absolutely not something that one does while watching a clock."

CHAPTER 15

The Wrecking Ball &
A Rite Of Passage

If you can fill the unforgiving minute
With sixty seconds' worth of distance run,
Yours is the Earth and everything that's in it,
And — which is more — you'll be a Man, my son!
                                    Rudyard Kipling
                        If: A Father's Advice to His Son

The seventies were a great era for rural America. International markets and prices were strong, the government made farmers a priority, and there were no real extreme weather events that challenged the harvest. Cotton and soybean farming evolved. Dad was always a late adopter, several years behind the curve. New trends allowed small farmers to become medium-sized farmers, and the medium-sized farmers started resembling the plantation owners of old. Average acreages grew from four or five hundred acres to well over a thousand. New equipment and farm practices helped producers keep up with their own growth. But many were mortgaged beyond their means.

When the 1980 drought hit, many families missed an entire year's income. The number of farmers nationwide that year decreased by a third and it began a downward agricultural spiral across the United States. Four years later, Willie Nelson, John Mellencamp, and Neil Young organized an event they called Farm Aid in Champaign, Illinois raising $9 million for farmers in danger of losing their land to mortgage debt. There were years when my father hid six-figure debt from my mother. That's the kind of money it takes to put a crop in the ground, especially when you carry debt from one year to the next. Her discovery of his enormous financial obligations on more than one occasion created some of the most difficult hardships two people can endure. Had it not been for her teaching career, a steady income, and an unwavering commitment to family, he never would have enjoyed his second chance at a good life past year five. It's been said that behind every farmer is a successful wife who works in town. The family landscape around Highbanks Road would tell you that's true enough.

For a farmer, there is nothing — no high-horsepowered equipment, no fertile land tract, no rebate check — more valuable than a son. That's not a sexist stereotype. It's just true. Male offspring on the farm is the equivalent of a good ten years' free labor. Indentured servitude begins with a hoe, and usually ends years later with a skilled tough-as-nails laborer ready for his own operation, or a young man who feels his dues are paid and is ready to leave that world behind.

When you put two men with polar-opposite personalities in an intense farm situation raising a crop year after year, one of two things will happen. They will become forever friends and partners dependent on each another for life, or they will count the days until they go their separate ways. My dad got a solid ten years' service from me right up to my first day of college. It was the one I'd always looked toward as my day of independence, with no looking back. One hundred forty-eight miles to the University of Central Arkansas wasn't far, but it was the precise distance to my freedom.

Growing and picking cotton and soybeans and the manual labor of tractor driving sounds easy, but there's a lot to learn on the farm environment. A bad decision can get farmers and hired hands hurt, even killed. The downside for us was that Dad was a terrible and impatient teacher, and I was a student who had no real interest in learning. Our first year working together was the drought year. Aside from his proclivity to procrastinate, which always put our work in a rush and behind, I watched my father grow completely helpless in 1980. The heat, no rain, and a complete unavailability of solutions to do anything about it nearly killed him as he watched a crop wither and die. The experience made a huge impression and left me wondering why I'd ever subject myself to so many circumstances beyond my control. In 1980, I made the personal decision that I'd be the first in five generations to leave the farm —unheard of back then for an only son.

I remember the day I became a man. There was no formal ceremony. Just a confrontation with a swearing fit in a sweltering gumbo field.

My father was not a man you challenged. He would call your bluff every time, then punish you for the idea of a confrontation. And he was especially good at this with those weaker than him. Mostly out of fear of conflict, I was a kid who would put up with a lot, and for a long time, until the tension got so high I was like a pressure cooker gauge in the red. That's why his unusual reaction to a complete meltdown I experienced one hot July day in 1982 remains so vivid in my memory.

The crop looked good that year, and the cotton and soybeans were tall enough now that you didn't want to run a tractor through the row middles. It was a labor-intensive year and we'd spent many hundred-hour weeks getting a good crop ready for harvest. All my friends were enjoying time around swimming pools and other leisure activities. Most of the other farm families were even taking time for a week off at the lake. No time off is the price a farmer pays when he's unorganized and a poor manager of his own schedule. My dad decided that he and I would end the summer big-weeding soybeans armed with a hoe and a jug of tepid ice water.

In late Arkansas summer, the difference in the air and ground temperatures often creates a heavy dew on everything that's exposed. The leaf hairs on a soybean leaf retain extra water until about 10 AM when the sun bears down, beginning the most intense heat of the day for the next six hours. Sultry. Oppressive. Sweltering. Choose whatever word you like. The air becomes so thick that your clothes carry an extra ten pounds as if they'd just come from the washing machine. The heat is an extra layer of misery when you're already exhausted from months of tending a crop.

We chopped along, not speaking much. Frustration mounted as I silently contemplated my friends lounging on Norfork Lake pontoons and taking afternoon naps in the air conditioning. It had been a wet year that prevented long stretches of herbicide applications with a heavy tractor, so there was an abundance of cockleburrs, teaweeds, and long morning glory vines. About then, I hit an extra-hard lick at a cockle burr stalk causing my hoe handle to snap in half. Dad looked at me in an accusatory manner as if I'd done it on purpose.

"I guess you can finish out the day with a broken hoe," he said, pulling some morning glory vines to the row middle.

That's when something inside me snapped, like that hoe handle.

"I've taken orders from you all summer long, worked as hard as any grown man could work, never complained, and I'm exhausted!" I yelled, looking directly into his eyes. "I don't know another fourteen-year-old kid in this country who works as hard as I do. You want to chop this field, you chop it yourself. I'm going home!" My lips moved, but there was no control over the words coming out.

With that unprecedented challenge to my father's authority, I threw the half hoe in his direction and it rolled to his feet. Then I began the mile-long walk home. Never looking back, I expected a tackle from behind and what would most likely be the beating of my life. My actions moments earlier were the first time I'd spoken to him as an equal. It was a defining moment where I left childhood behind, so a fist fight and Dad putting me back in my place was likely in order. It never happened, and I cried in a raging fit the entire way, plodding through hot sun. Classic farm boy meltdown.

Thirty minutes later, muddy streams of tears on my cheeks, I stormed through the house straight to my room and lay down on the bed, some pressure relieved, but awaiting the inevitable. It was inconceivable what I'd just done.

An hour passed. Finally, footsteps coming down the hallway, and the door carefully creaked open. He sat on the bed beside me and put his arm around my neck as I began crying again, this time as much from fear as anger. "I want to tell you something."

"You've worked hard this summer and I'm sorry I never tell you how much I appreciate it. I want you to go in there and take a shower and take the rest of the week off. Come back to work on Monday, but go rest and have some fun for now. I'm sorry, okay?"

It was the first time I'd heard those words. Ever. And with that, he walked out of the house and back to the field intent on finishing the job we'd started.

My God, he's human after all.

CHAPTER 16

Lord, Bring A Hurricane

All we got is the family unbroke.

John Steinbeck
The Grapes of Wrath

There is no formal rite of passage, no elaborate celebration, no grand ceremony when a young boy in rural America becomes old enough to drive a two-hundred horsepower piece of farm equipment. One day I was chopping cotton in the scalding heat cursing my existence at the end of a nine-dollar hoe. The next, I was at the wheel of a hundred-thousand-dollar rig with dual wheels driving monotonously across hundreds of acres a day. There is no fanfare, but a cab tractor with an AM/FM radio and air-conditioning beats the hoe handle any day.

On the cusp of the busy season in June 1979, my father decided it was a better day for drinking beer than cutting wheat. As the morning sun quickly dried flowing wheat fields across the countryside, we moved the necessary parade of harvest equipment to an eighty-acre patch that was ready to go. Around noon, he put me in a combine cab for the first time ever, barked a few instructions, and turned over to me one of the most complicated pieces of equipment in the farm inventory. I was thirteen. His pre-harvest pep talk was more threat than lesson, but without knowing it he shared an important life lesson that day.

My dad taught me how to listen.

Any machine designed for harvesting crops, whether grain or fiber, is a complex assemblage of thousands of moving parts. They are designed for cutting, shelling, separating product from waste, raising and lifting, temporary storage and distribution. When a combine or cotton picker is doing its job it's not unlike a well-practiced orchestra, each section coming in perfectly at the right moment, never missing a beat, and not a note off key. A farmer who knows what he's listening for can detect a problem immediately, shut the operation down, and often fix a small problem before it becomes a ten-thousand-dollar repair job.

"You run one of these machines with your ears," my dad said, hovering over me in the dusty cab. "You hear one thing that doesn't sound normal and you shut her down. She's all yours."

With that, he retired to the turn row, where he sat on a pickup truck tailgate for the day with his buddy, Doyle Yates, consuming one cold Budweiser after another from a Styrofoam cooler.

I cut almost fifty acres of wheat over the next ten hours, and took from it a lesson I've used in both family and career. There is all the difference in the world between hearing and listening. Hearing is passive. What you *hear* mostly is noise. Things get more specific, and they have more meaning and more context when you listen. It requires intent. You work at listening. You hear the words people say, but if you listen closely enough, it evolves to discernment, and the communication takes on a whole new dimension.

Today, I run a five-horsepower push lawnmower with the same intent as those big farm machines from thirty-five years ago. And in conversation, I can sense what people are communicating, even if they don't say it well. Understanding my father required a lot of heavy listening, especially to all the things not said.

By the next year, Dad was almost ten years into his farming career. With the exception of the kickstart from his mother-in-law, who'd rented him two hundred acres getting started, he'd done things mostly on his own and with a big assist from Mom's teaching career. My mother's salary gave him the luxury of stable income. But he had become a more productive farmer with a decent reputation for clean crops and straight rows. He was a five-hundred-acre farmer now, and yields were consistently average to good. I was his full-time staff of one. When school ended in mid-May, there were no family vacations to the lake, no afternoon visits to the community swimming pool, no baseball games. We worked.

That year also forevermore changed cotton farming communities like Highbanks.

As late as Memorial Day, 1980 showed prospects for another year that would give the farm community enough money to make a living and grow family operations a bit. The problems began in June when a ridge of high pressure settled into the lower Mississippi Valley and camped for four months. Temperatures exceeded a hundred degrees for thirty-three consecutive days and it rained less than one-tenth of an inch through September. The heat wave caused seventeen hundred deaths, and losses in the agricultural community amounted to $61 billion.

There's not a more helpless feeling than watching Mother Nature claim thousands of dollars a day. Each morning, my father vomited violently in the privacy of his bathroom. He would emerge watery-eyed and pre-occupied, each day thinner than the next from no appetite.

You can always pray. And families did just that. Local weather forecasters said the prevailing high pressure causing the drought was so strong, it would take a hurricane strike on the Gulf Coast to break it. There were church services in 1980 dedicated to that very thing. Our church community prayed for a hurricane, and eventually we got one. But by the time hurricane Allen made its way through the Caribbean and hit south Texas, it was too late. Much of the brittle cotton and soybeans went unharvested as the cost of fuel would have exceeded the yield. Many friends and family shut down their farm operations altogether. Others went even deeper in debt investing in irrigation systems that radically changed the farm landscape forever. Our family rolled indebtedness over from one year to the next, still hundreds of thousands of dollars in debt at Dad's retirement almost twenty years later. An exorbitant life insurance policy they struggled to pay year after year was all that ultimately saved the farm. In my father's death, he literally bought the farm.

TURN ROW

The Arkansas Delta — part of what is referred to as the Lower Mississippi River Valley, the Mississippi embayment or the Mississippi River Alluvial Plain — formed twelve thousand years ago as the Mississippi River and its tributaries eroded older deposits and built up new, deep layers of soil, gravel, and clay. It washed the sediment from as far west as the slopes of the Rocky Mountains southward to the present-day Gulf of Mexico. Over the millennia, the slow soil transfer has created an alluvial plain extending two hundred and fifty miles north and south, and anywhere from twelve miles wide to ninety-one miles at its broadest. Along with certain regions in China, Brazil, and California's Central Valley, it's known as one of the world's most productive agricultural regions. You're hard pressed to find a more naturally suited environment for growing cotton and rice.

In the centuries that followed the massive soil transfer, tree varieties including cypress, tupelo, gum, oak, and willow grew dense in the lowlands, giving birth to one of the largest wetland regions in the United States. Frontiersmen and prospective farmers cleared the bottomland hardwoods over time, destroying seventy percent of the wetlands. The Big Lake National Wildlife Refuge just across the county line is one of the few remaining examples of the original environment.

The landscape is one that captures a scene as far as your eyes can focus. Its elevations are almost non-existent, ranging between one hundred and three hundred feet above sea level.

As the new world continued its expansion westward, it was only a hundred miles south in the Delta's southern tip where in 1686 the French settled the first commercial trading establishment west of the Mississippi on the banks of the lower Arkansas River. In 1815, Arkansas Post became the location from which explorers set out to survey the Louisiana Purchase, a moment in history signaling the end of the territory's French and Spanish dominance, and their trade relationship with the Quapaw. The Post became the first capital of the Arkansas Territory in 1819.

In its modern two hundred and twenty year history, the Delta has shaped a people who are not immune to catastrophe and hardship. It is a peaceful land, but one subject to any variety of natural calamity.

From December 1811 to February 1812, the New Madrid Fault, which extends a hundred and fifty miles north to south from Cairo, Illinois to Marked Tree, Arkansas, unleashed a series of earthquakes, still the most powerful ever to hit the continental United States east of the Rockies. Several ranged in magnitude from (M 7.5–7.9). While there was little loss of life amongst a sparse population, structural damage to property was widespread as the soil reportedly liquefied and rolled in repeated, tumbling waves more than it shook. In nearby Lake County, Tennessee, a twenty-square mile area caved in on itself and caused the nearby Mississippi River to backfill the depression as it flowed backwards for days. Newspaper reports said the biggest quake caused church bells to ring in Boston. Today, seismologists say the New Madrid zone is past due for another major shift.

The worst maritime disaster in United States history unfolded just sixty miles south in late April 1865, just eighteen days after the end of the Civil War. As a steamship called Sultana transported now released Union soldiers north to St. Louis, one of its four boilers blew and she burned to the waterline near Marion, Arkansas. the ship was designed to carry three hundred seventy six passengers. She was loaded that day with almost five times her capacity. Almost twelve hundred passengers died in the calamity. The news was overshadowed and the history practically lost as the event occurred on the same day as President Abraham Lincoln's assassination. Meanwhile, bodies were found downriver for months.

From 1999 to 2001, and during the heart of my career as a newspaper journalist, I made it a tradition each new year's day to interview my grandmother (my mom's mother) on camera, capturing her thoughts about life and the historical events she'd witnessed across almost ninety years in a rural community she never left.

One of the moments she most vividly recalled was her experience during the 1918 influenza epidemic, that killed more people worldwide than any disease outbreak in human history. The 1918 flu, eventually known as the Spanish flu, killed more people in a year than the Black Death did in a century. Even in the relatively remote area of the Delta and eastern Arkansas, thousands were lost.

My grandmother was a nine-year-old child that year, and the only one of her eight-member family, including the parents, who was spared the illness. She became nursemaid to all, scouring the country for corn whiskey — the closest thing available that resembled any medications — and stayed up long nights with critically ill, coughing children. Not one person in the household was lost.

It became so cold that winter, she recalled, that the ground froze deep enough to prevent burials until the following spring. Frozen bodies were stacked in churches and barns around the countryside for months.

In the spring of 1927, warm weather and early snow melts in Canada caused the upper Mississippi to swell. Rain fell in the upper Midwest, sending its full rivers gushing into the already swollen Mississippi. Its destination, the Gulf of Mexico, acted as a stopper when it too became full. Then, in the South, it began to rain.

Arkansas saw record rainfall during April and with lakes, rivers, and stream beds full, there was no place the water could go. The Mississippi backed up into tributary rivers including the Arkansas, White, and St. Francis, essentially making the Mississippi as much as sixty miles wide in some places. It remained above flood stage one hundred and fifty three days. Two million acres of farmland flooded and three hundred and fifty thousand residents were displaced, mostly to one of eighty Red Cross Camps along the Delta. Dead animals floated everywhere. National Geographic magazine said when seven inches of rain fell in Little Rock over two hours, "the streets were dry and dusty at noon, but by 2 PM, mules were drowning on Main Street faster than people could unhitch them from wagons."

Just three years later in 1930, the region was still recovering when the same rich farmland that was submerged for months turned to dust and blew away in drought.

As in most disasters, the 1927 flood saw the best and the worst of humanity. Of the 1927 flood, author John Barry said in *Rising Tide*: "Their struggle...began as one of man against nature. It became one of man against man. Honor and money collided. White and black collided. Regional and national power structures collided. The collisions shook America."

CHAPTER 17

Country Folk

The best thing about a small town is that you grow up knowing everyone.
  It's also the worst thing.

Pat Conroy

There were two kinds of people in the Highbanks Road community: all the ones who knew your business and looked on you as a sinner worse than themselves, and the ones who knew all your sins and loved you just the same. Word traveled fast in a community where most telephones were connected on a four-home party line. The stories got even juicier as they got retold in the town coffee shop, barber shop, and beauty shop. And on Sunday, everyone was thankful the preacher delivered the weekly message with a bit of hellfire and brimstone because the family sitting next to them needed the corrective word so badly.

Across the United States, there is no better place to find juicy, highly exaggerated gossip than in a coffee shops where men gather in rural America. It was my dad's experience with one of the community's toughest characters in the summer of 1983 that kept him away from the coffee shop ridicule for three months.

That character was Elmer Duncan, and the best strategy for getting along with Elmer was just walking in the other direction. Narrow waist, broad shoulders, chiseled face, weathered skin, and long, blonde hair that he combed frequently, Elmer was forever young like a Greek god. He worked as a tractor-driving hired hand from one place to another, a temper so bad he never lasted long in a single place. He relished his bad-boy role in a standard uniform seven days a week — Levi jeans and a sleeveless, ribbed t-shirt (they called it a wife-beater in those days). When you saw him out cruising the dirt roads in his restored early model Chevy pickup, Elmer was most likely drinking, and depending on the week he'd had, possibly looking for a fight.

This is not the kind of man for whom my father had great affinity. He hated a cocky soul.

The men and women who lead American farm families are some of the best people you'll ever know. They are moral, hardworking, generous, welcoming, and unpretentious. And they are generally mild-mannered with the exception of a few weeks in June when circumstances come together for a perfect storm of stress-induced emotion. It's the farm frenzy, a two- to three-week period when there's a harvest, replanting, and ongoing work to keep the existing crops clean. It's like being all-in at the poker table. Everything rides on the circumstances, and twenty-four hours is too short a day. Everyone's tired, ready for a break, and on edge. I've seen farmers who were deacons at First Baptist Church go on a cussing tirade in the summer rush. And David Watkins was no church deacon.

It was on a late Saturday afternoon during this time when my father walked into the house looking as if he'd fallen off some mountaintop. Busted lip, left eye swollen shut, and deep, bloody scrapes everywhere else, he was like a tomcat home from a three-week countryside prowl. He wasn't angry, or even highly agitated. Just desperately in need of some first aid. With an appearance that betrayed him, there was no way he could get around telling the story.

Headed home from the "Corner Farm," Dad was driving a tractor with a six-row cultivator in tow, and Elmer was oncoming in his prized blue Chevy. Any set of circumstances can make it difficult for a farmer to pull to the side, and country protocol is generally that the oncoming vehicle will do all it can to make easy passage. But Elmer wasn't interested in protocol. He wanted to hold his side of the road putting Dad in an impossible position.

It was like striking a match to tinder.

Eyes dead set on one other, my father dismounted the tractor, and Elmer exited the blue Chevy not even bothering to close the door. Intently, they walked straight toward each another, no exchange of words necessary. It was a season when my dad was fifty, overweight, and over-confident, and Elmer was in the prime of his meanness and his physical toughness. Of course, that never crossed Dad's mind. All reason goes out the window when two men like this are just looking for a fight.

Two country gladiators they were, both intent on teaching the other guy a serious lesson. As they met, Elmer threw a sharp right jab square to my father's left eye. It put him on the ground immediately. Dazed, he got up, ran toward Elmer again, and managed to wrestle him to the ground. From there, Elmer got on top of him and beat him just enough so that he knew he'd been in a fight. It was over before it started. If anything, I always appreciated that Elmer didn't kill him.

Predictably, in the months that followed, my father never once regretted the fight — that he could have been killed, that it was poor judgment, or that it was an embarrassment to the family. What he most lamented was that he didn't get off the tractor carrying a three-quarter-inch wrench. It was a small miracle he didn't. One of the two would have never walked away.

Events like this become stories of legend in the morning coffee shops. And the more the story's subject does to avoid the crowd, the taller the tales become. Dad was a regular at Dixie Bennet's coffee shop. He stayed away for three months. That's how bad he looked.

Several years later, Elmer Duncan was speeding ninety miles an hour down the highway when he swerved his motorcycle to dodge some roadkill. He lost control, flipped end over end, and they said his body rolled violently down the asphalt pavement for more than a hundred yards. They picked him up in pieces so there would be something for the coffin.

The men in the community were a colorful cast of characters. For every young boy who grew up along Highbanks Road, a little piece of each one lives inside him.

We had three JDs, three JLs, two Curlies, and two Peewees, the youngest of which is still famous for his 1974 streaking run all the way from Wooten's Gas Station to the stoplight when he was seventeen years old. He would have gone farther, but witnesses said he just gave plum out. Bad luck for Peewee, the beating his father administered afterward surpassed the legend of the original story.

There were more Juniors than you could count. Our neighbor, Junior Bibb bought a brand-new pickup truck every January. Tommy Swetnam earned the moniker "Tee Hee" for his funny little laugh. JD and Gene Gibbons were brothers and farm partners who frequently got in drunken fights. One was so bad the summer of 1982 that JD nearly drowned Gene in a mud puddle six inches deep. Witnesses said the brouhaha ended only because they were overweight, exhausted, and ran out of fighting steam. When it was over, they both lay in the mud recovering and sobering up for a good hour, most likely having forgotten what started it in the first place.

If it flowed from the tongue just right, we'd call people by their given and family names. Billy Ray Gibbons ran Red Onion liquor store. Bobby Joe Pitts farmed cotton and loved duck hunting. Claude Earl Barnett was the town's go-to man for automotive parts.

Van Ray Hamilton was a lovable carpenter with an affinity for cheap whiskey, but he wasn't the sharpest stick in the room. When a group of his misfit friends, led by my dad, got wind that Van Ray's sitting hen was about to hatch chicks, they watched closely and dyed the chicks every color of the rainbow before he got his first look. Ecstatic with the anomaly, Van Ray thought himself destined for fame and fortune with his rainbow chicks until the dye wore off days later. He forever believed the chicks naturally hatched that way.

Norma Sue Gathright was the sweetest Sunday school teacher who ever lived. If a woman's middle name was Sue or Lou, chances were high she had a double moniker, and she probably made out-of-this-world banana pudding, too.

Norma Sue's clan, the Gathright boys, had an annual farm shop bash on the first day of dove season each September that drew bigshots from across the territory. Big Jack headed up the event. Gene "The Governor," our local justice of the peace, and his son, Redworm, were always present. Grubworm, Dennis, and Alan Gathright were there, too, as was Peewee, the streaker. Next to Christmas and Thanksgiving, there wasn't a day more highly anticipated than dove season opening day. But it was much more about cold beer and barbecue than hunting doves.

In the early '80s, some young men in the only neighboring town with a golf course got the bright idea to host a tournament on opening day — a redneck biathlon of sorts. They added an interesting twist, illegally baiting the nine greens with wheat seed. Within twenty-four hours, the course was covered in game birds. Most tournament participants packed a .12 gauge in their bag alongside fairway woods and irons for a golf tournament and dove hunt combo event. Throw in dozens of coolers with cold beer and you have yourself a real fiasco with rednecks on golf carts running around shooting firearms at anything that moves.

Bad news for all was that federal game wardens got wind of the scheme days in advance. People there said when they raided the event, golf carts scattered in twenty directions. Some made it home. Others were not so lucky. The game and fish authorities made examples of several, banning their hunting privileges forever. It's the most severe penalty you can exact on just about any man in this part of the world. Take his gun away and you might as well chisel off an arm.

There were good men in the community who with honorable intentions ended their lives too soon. Some who were diagnosed with terminal illness ended their lives to spare their families the long-term care and grief. Others, who battled the chronic depression that comes with farm life, lost their sense of sound judgment because of wrongly prescribed drugs and found their final moments holding a sawed-off shotgun to their head or putting a rope around their neck. This was the curse of the 1980s Farm Crisis — the shame of losing land that had been in the family for seven generations or more.

Wimp Harrell, who still lives near Highbanks Road today, was a respected farmer, as was Bruiser Bruce, one of Dad's favorite hunting partners. Harry "Double-Cola" Carle was an avid sportsman and single father who got caught up in a coupon redemption scheme serving several years in prison. He was doing what he could to provide for his family, and no one ever blamed him for that. As a boy, I frequently played cards with a gin worker named Dink Gadberry. Everyone loved and respected Mr. Gail Cullum for raising and lowering the flag at the Legion Hut every day. He was one of the best of the greatest generation.

For decades, Red Hot Cullum was the butcher at his brother's store, Noble's Grocery, where I bought my first pack of Salem Light cigarettes. I eventually became part of a golf sixsome with Red, and we played frequently at Big Lake Country Club. In all his decades on that course, Red was famous for a single shot off the number six tee, a one-hundred-nineteen-yard par three, where he skulled his tee shot, rolling it all the way up and onto the green. (This shot is often referred to as a worm burner.) Witnesses watched in amazement as the ball ascended the green and broke hard left, winding down toward the cup and in. Old men slapped high fives like kids, celebrating the shot as if picture perfect. No points for style, but Red got his ace, and later that day true to custom, he bought drinks for everyone in the clubhouse.

The golf rounds were especially fun when family friend, and Red's best friend, Jay Mays, would visit from Troy, Illinois on long weekends. He was one of the most likable men you'd ever know, so cool and so essential to the group we lovingly and respectfully called him The Boy from Troy. We lost Jay to cancer in 2014. Good times were never the same.

The ladies around Highbanks Road and the Buffalo Island community took an interest in helping raise children far beyond those in their immediate family. Pug Wimberley, Verna Lou Harrell and Norma Sue Gathright were all godmothers to me, the essence of angels on earth. Their husbands should have worshiped the ground they walked on.

I never met them, but there were twin sisters just across Caney Slough named Toots and Beans. They were part of a legion of women known as the Crockpot Brigade who supplied home-cooked food at special church events and funerals. Toots and Beans were famous for the unique spice cakes they baked in old Folgers coffee cans, preparing them for distribution at the nursing homes each Christmas.

Margaret Reed was one of the most intriguing women around. For years you could hear her reading the news and advertisements on local radio station KBIB 1560 AM. Margaret was a German native who came to the United States with new husband Jerry Reed just after the Korean War. Wonderful lady, but I never understood how she got hired as a radio announcer in rural Arkansas. No one ever understood a single word she said on air.

That's what made the area around Highbanks Road such an interesting place to grow up. Everyone had a story. I spent a lot of my own adult years wondering if I should have spent more time getting to know my own father's.

TURN ROW

Draw a hundred-mile radius around Highbanks Road and you'll find a surprising number of high-profile people with roots in the land.

Best-selling author John Grisham was born in Jonesboro and wrote about rural farm life in his book, *A Painted House*. The Piggott community, just north, was home to Ernest Hemingway's second wife, Pauline Pfeiffer, and it was there where he penned a substantial portion of the classic *A Farewell to Arms*.

The land is rich in native musicians who enjoyed success including Sheryl Crow, Johnny Cash, and Buddy Jewel. Charlie Rich and Rev. Al Green grew up in St. Francis County within miles of one another, and just down the road from future heavyweight champion Sonny Liston. Brothers Doug and Ricky Phelps, who had roots in their father's Assembly of God Church in Monette, hit it big as members of The Kentucky Headhunters in 1989 with smash hits, *Walk Softly on this Heart of Mine*, and *Dumas Walker*.

In September 1964, en route to a private retreat before their final US concert that year, the Beatles created a mob-like frenzy with a surprise landing where they changed planes at the Walnut Ridge airport. A documentary, *Liverpool, Abbey Road and Walnut Ridge* records the fleeting history locals still celebrate.

Mary Steenburgen and Wes Bentley are two Broadway and motion picture stars with ties to the land, Bentley the son of Rev. David Bentley who led the Monette Methodist Church for two years. Ben Murphy, co-star of the early 70s television series *Alias Smith & Jones* spent considerable time at his grandmother's home on Highbanks Road. It was about that same time when a southern rock band called Black Oak, Arkansas reached the height of its fame.

Ever stayed at a Holiday Inn? Founder Kemmons Wilson was born in Osceola near the banks of the Mississippi River. In Newport, US Senator Kaneaster Hodges frequently hosted President Jimmy Carter for duck hunts on the White River. Monette native Kent Cullum is a world-champion duck caller several times over.

In the spring of 1983, Lawrence County made national headlines in the "Smithville Shootout." Sheriff Gene Matthews and North Dakota farmer Gordon Kahl both died from wounds sustained in a massive FBI takedown operation on the training grounds of a group known as Posse Comitatus. Kahl was on the run for months claiming the U.S. government operated under a communist manifesto and the obligation to pay federal taxes violated his religious principles.

Just an hour and fifteen minute drive south on Interstate 55 and you'll find a place Elvis Presley called Graceland.

CHAPTER 18

Fish Fries & Barbecues

And when my life is through, bury me in barbecue, but make sure it's vinegar based, 'cause you know that slows decay, and it's the style from our home state ...

Rhett & Link
The BBQ Song

Eating fresh seafood in the Arkansas Delta does not mean you're about to enjoy a flaky plate of red snapper, succulent buttered lobster tails, or a steaming bowl of shrimp étouffée over rice. What it means is that you and the family are headed to the local catfish cafe, every small town's Saturday night hot spot.

Seafood in these parts is a sizzling plate of perfectly fried catfish filets with tartar sauce on the side, crunchy hush puppies, French fries, and beer-battered onion rings. A chilled bowl of rightly seasoned coleslaw and pickled green tomatoes cuts the grease and keeps you going back for more.

Some wouldn't feed catfish to their hunting dog. They're likely the same ones who enjoy things like caviar and goose liver pâté. But if it ever gets into your belly just once, that fleshy white fish, fried perfectly with salt and corn meal, becomes something you crave on a frequent basis. "Fish hungry," they call it, a country urge that just won't go away until it's satisfied.

Local diners and cafes are the quick fix to a fish-hungry predicament. For decades, one restaurateur held revered-institution status with his famous tagline *Sixty-Two Feet of All You Can Eat*. It was a veritable cornucopia of deep-fried starch and gluten, and on Friday nights the line out the door was longer than the buffet. What you'll most likely enjoy in these cafes is the pond-raised commercial catfish variety grown somewhere nearby. The Mississippi Delta is the capital of the commercial catfish industry.

But in the off-season or on a rainy day when there's more time on hand, a down-home fish fry in the farm shop with friends from all around is a great way to pass a day. There is but one code that applies to the fish fries around Highbanks Road: *all are welcome*.

It most often begins with heating several gallons of pure lard to a sizzle. Home-made fish fryers built by some of the countryside's best welders are as common as the sunrise, their predominant feature a several-gallon vat that sits over a collection of gas burners that look powerful enough to launch a space shuttle. Once the grease is hot and the fresh-caught fish are thawed, it's easy. Hushpuppies, onion rings, and fries go first, followed by the fish most usually cut as a bone-in steak. Old-timers actually prefer the taste of bone-in catfish claiming it enhances the unique river flavor. Yes, you can taste the river in these fish. Some call it an acquired taste.

But for every fish fry across the Arkansas Delta landscape, you'll find ten barbecues. There is a spicy mix of vinegar and paprika in our blood that dates to the earliest plantations where African-American slaves introduced the slow-cook method for meats that no one else thought edible.

If you're going to say something bad about a person's barbecue here, you might as well go ahead and mention his mama's fat thighs and the way she sings off key each Sunday in the last stanza of *Just As I Am*. Barbecue is a serious and prideful business in the Delta.

Careless words? Nope. Them's fightin' words.

Most people believe the key to good barbecue is some secret ingredient or recipe handed down through the generations that stays buried in a Mason jar somewhere out in the chicken yard. Truth is, it's not the sauce, or the seasonings, or even the meat itself that makes good barbecue.

The secret to great barbecue is patience, time, and regulated heat that come together for something we call *low and slow*.

Some say it was a dear old grandfatherly man in a white suit and black Kentucky tie who invented the *extra crispy* food concept. But is just isn't true.

David Watkins was neither patient, nor did he know how to build a charcoal fire that would ever slip below an inferno level of six hundred degrees. It's hard believing how a fifty-gallon drum could hold so much heat. Charcoal or gas, it mattered not. The more lighter fluid you could apply, the better, Dad thought. He could turn the finest meats into blackened, dry, shoe leather in five minutes. The aftertaste was a delicate blend of ashen wood and petroleum.

He loved it all the more when the gas grill became popular. You could go from cold grill to hellishly hot in seconds and cook a burger in two minutes even if it did bleed out in the middle.

It took thirty years to unlearn everything the man ever showed me about barbecue. But did he ever love playing the role of Saturday afternoon grill master.

His signature move was slathering the meat with cheap sauce, high in sugar content, throughout the process. Bad thing is, high temperatures, charcoal, and sugar rarely mix well. Instead of a moist, finger-licking seasoning that compliments the meat, what's left behind is a black, crunchy, caramelized ash, hard enough you almost have to crack the meat open. Lick your fingers of this ashen residue and it will make you choke. The surgeon general has issued warnings against products less harmful.

But the pictures of him enjoying his bounty are forever emblazoned in my mind. In his standard seat at our three-person family kitchen bar, utensil etiquette was checked at the front door. With both hands, he'd take a leathery pork steak to his mouth, or perhaps a bone-dry chicken breast, and close his eyes savoring the first fruits. "Lord, ain't that good," he'd say, complimenting himself and never really looking at anyone. It was as if he'd just tasted the most succulent poultry dish offered by a three-star Michelin bouchon. The remains always proved his whole-hearted belief. A smooth, perfectly picked pile of bones covered his plate, and chances were good he'd also gnawed a minute or two on what you left behind.

His lack of patience and proclivity toward the things that offered immediate gratification were also the ironic barrier to my dad's understanding of his own forgiveness. He was a man from a long line of men who lived by their senses. He believed in what he could see, what he could hear, and especially what he could feel in the moment. These physical senses are our toughest barriers to faith.

There is a moment in the Christian life that changes everything. It's not the ritual of baptism, praying a prayer, or kneeling at any altar. These are simply acts of obedience and testimony. It's not some moment wrapped around a comprehensive understanding of God — because of God's nature as one who is omniscient, omnipotent, and omnipresent, that never really happens. How can we comprehend the incomprehensible?

It is a simple, authentic, childlike, from-the-heart decision that unleashes the currency of the Kingdom. It comes in our first step of faith.

Most of his life, Dad never rejoiced in his forgiveness, because he couldn't feel it, and because he never chased the meaning of his own faith.

What he was looking for was the magic moment that would come without the wait. He wanted the epiphany. The grand revelation of forgiveness. Who of us can blame another for their wish to feel forgiven?

How that faith ultimately came to him is indeed a gospel miracle performed by an uncompromising God with an imminent will.

CHAPTER 19

Trot Lines & 'Talfy Worms

Many of the most highly publicized events of my presidency are not nearly as memorable or significant in my life as fishing with my daddy.

Jimmy Carter

During the times when we were the luckiest, there was always a young buck in our fishing crew who was skinny enough, and crazy or drunk enough, to shimmy up into the tree's highest branches, climb out on each one, the further the better, and give them a good shake as he worked his way down.

In late July, they'll fall to the ground by the thousands, wriggling and wiggling back toward the broad green tree leaves they instinctively gorge upon. In such massive populations they emit a pungent, half-minty, half-sour kind of scent. They are so desired, in such high demand, that as the first sightings are made in treetops along the back country roads, the news spreads faster than if the preacher's wife just ran off with the constable.

The elusive catalpa worm (or catalfy, shortened even further by most old-timers to 'talfy worm) is so treasured as the perfect catfish bait that old men and enterprising children will collect them by the five-gallon buckets and freeze them inside ziplock bags for outings in the months ahead. Kids become seasonal entrepreneurs gathering them in pint jars and selling them for cash. For those stored in the freezer, it's important to include a few dozen leaves. Rural legend has it they'll wake up hungrier than ever during the slow thaw and resume munching away as if nothing ever happened.

The emergence of the catalpa worm in late July and early August coincides with the brief few days the agriculture community is winding down before harvest. It is the unofficial season for trot lining, and it was one of my father's favorite pastimes.

Trot lining is a simple, uncomplicated, even passive method for catching certain fish species. And it's crazy effective when the bite is on. The practice involves nothing more than a heavy line tied at both banks of a river channel, a few weights and gallon-milk jugs, and drop lines with baited hooks every yard or so. There are seasoned river veterans who are deadly serious about it, and those, like my dad, who enjoyed the thrill a couple of times a year. As a double bonus, Dad got to drink beer and stay out late at night catching fish, and each successful outing assured future fish fries where there would be more beer drinking and carrying on.

In late summer, the St. Francis River channels gradually lower as much as ten or twelve feet down the banks, creating perfect conditions for trot lining and several coolers full of channel cat, blue, and the occasional flathead. There are as many great legends of "river monsters" that got away as there are venues where these bottom-lurking scavengers thrive, but the facts speak for them-

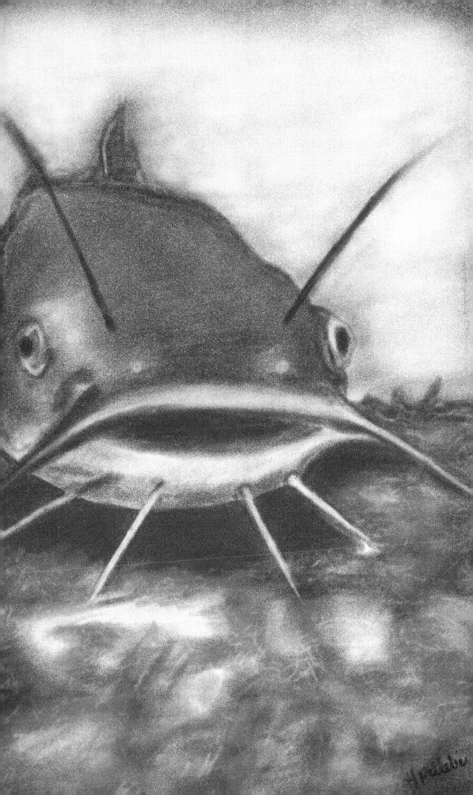

selves. Documented Arkansas records include a thirty-eight-pound channel cat out of Lake Ouachita, an eighty-pound flathead from the Arkansas River, and a one-hundred-seventy-pound blue harvested from the Mississippi River. The blue, in excess of five feet long, put up a forty-five minute fight before the angler brought him along boat side. Exponentially bigger than the dip net on hand, a small team of men wrestled the leviathan into a capture. It remains an all-tackle world record today, a one-hundred-seventy-pound monster caught on twenty-pound test line. The secret bait that got the big one? A can of Spam.

Among local sportsmen, trot lining is less of an art and science than duck hunting, and not quite as much of a party as the first day of dove season. I think Dad and his crew enjoyed the anticipation almost as much as the fishing. The day plays out something like this:

It takes two or more people to execute a successful trot lining expedition. One person navigates a flat-bottomed boat with an outboard motor. The other lays, baits, and checks the lines. Oftentimes, several teams come together for what is essentially an all-night, beer-drinking, fish-fest.

Tying lines and securing the bait occupies most of the afternoon. Depending on the number of lines that will get set, boats hit the river about an hour before dusk. With the late summer water levels now low along the bank, each end is typically tied to an exposed tree root system washed away by the current. Secured on both sides, the trotline now extends across the thirty- to forty-yard river channel at various depths. Depending on his beer intake to that point, the baiter and line setter will occasionally spit on a hook set or two for good luck. Dad must have said it to me a hundred times, if one. "There'll be a big 'un there when we get back."

Lines set, now all you can do is wait.

The serious fishermen go home at this point, catch three to four hours sleep, then return around midnight refreshed, alert, and ready for the action. Others, like Dad's crew, would spend the next four hours gathered around a fire at the landing whooping and hollering, telling tall tales and seeing how fast they could drain a twelve-ounce can. There is nothing quite like a crew of drunken trot liners navigating the river channels on a summer night.

Sometime around midnight, it's time to run the lines. Pitch dark now, that means slowly navigating the boat up-current by way of a battery-powered floodlight. Beyond illuminating the channel, the floodlight portrays the reality of exactly where you are.

Moths and mosquitoes are drawn to the light so thick you can barely see much else. In all shapes and sizes, they come right at the light's source, some as big as birds, others so frightful they look like something straight out of the Mesozoic Era. Mosquitoes relentlessly attack every inch of exposed skin and instinctively head straight for your ears, nose, and mouth. In the quiet waters, you can hear the assailants and know you're in the midst of a blood-sucking legion. It's an experience that gets everybody sobered up inside the first ten minutes. These are the first critters that let you know you're on their turf.

It's not easy finding a nylon line tied to a sycamore root in the pitch of night and through a sea of insects. Easing along bank side, the person in front of the boat scours the shoreline slowly back and forth with the floodlight. As he does, a whole other world comes to life, this one ruled by the planet's only semiaquatic viper, prevalent throughout the southeastern quadrant of the continental United States. Their slitted, cat-like eyes reflect through the tree roots and against the bright light, a serpentine devil capable of striking a venomous, potentially fatal blow with venom glands so large their jowls protrude to create a triangular head. Aggressive when provoked or disturbed in their habitat, they spread their fangs in a wide, threatening display, revealing the white mouth that gives them the moniker *cottonmouth*. Gliding atop the water and slithering among the tree roots and logs along the shoreline, it is easy to imagine a cottonmouth doing its best to get into the boat with you. Also known as water moccasins, they will instinctively wrap their arm-thick bodies around the same root where a trot line gets tied, or at least it always seemed so. Checking the line means motoring right up to them and trying to shoo them away. *There is no boat paddle manufactured that is long enough for this job.* If the fishermen are lucky, there are still a few lingering effects from all the beer to help desensitize the very real danger.

A snake of any variety — venomous or not — is about the only thing that consistently made my father uneasy. His senior status in the duck blind always magically carried over into trot lining, so he was the one who ran the motor in back of the boat and away from all the slithering action. I sat mid-boat, as young as six, watching all this play out, and the images of thick moccasins wrapped around the tree roots still haunt occasional dreams.

With the near proximity clear of predators who would do you harm, it's time to run the line. This is an art in itself. It takes a steady hand pulling and maneuvering the trotline across a strong river current with sharp-as-a-razor #10 hooks dangling everywhere.

It doesn't take long knowing there's a fish on a drop line ahead. Catfish, even at two pounds, are powerful animals and will put up a fight until they're exhausted. Jerking and pulling on the line ahead, the line tender will call, "Fish on!" It brings hope for the same scenario several times over as the team works the line across the river run.

Seven, eight, ten-pound catfish are not uncommon in these circumstances. It takes a heap of strength to haul a ten-pound flathead into the boat from six feet down. Pulling him toward the surface you can only hope that he hasn't been there long enough that the alligator gar got to him. It's survival of the fittest in these river bottoms. If it can't move, or get away, it's food, especially to the prehistoric-looking gar.

There's nothing pretty about these bottom feeders. A flathead catfish is one of the ugliest creatures on the river. Safely in the boat bottom, they will periodically "growl" at the captor. Contrary to common belief, the whiskers on a catfish are perfectly harmless. It's the pectoral and dorsal fins just behind the head that will inject a toxin swelling hands and arms for days. Dad's forearms often swelled so tight it seemed they might burst.

Bring the fish in, re-bait the line, and check the remaining hooks. Some lines will catch as many as six or eight, sometimes the bite just isn't on. As the lines are checked and re-baited, there's more waiting time, and a final run again before dawn. If all goes well, there's a fish-cleaning party that will end around eight the next morning, then sleep. The exhausted, hungover fishermen will dream of boiling lard and that big fish fry just ahead.

TURN ROW

Nothing will get you more up close and personal with the water moccasins and alligator gar than an old catfishing technique that is purely man versus fish. The old timers call it hogging, or noodling.

This ancient method that dates back to the Native Americans and is still practiced by some purists today is one where the fisherman enters the water clinging to roots and vines remaining no more than an arm's length away from shore. As he holds tight with one hand, he uses his free hand to feel for the crevices and underwater caves where the big fish lurk, awaiting a crawdad snack or any potential victim that makes its way by. In the murky waters, a river monster will clamp down on a man's hand just as quickly as it will anything else it senses as food. *Yes, you are inviting and willingly allowing the carnivore fish to bite and swallow your hand.*

When it clinches down, the fisherman literally grabs the fish from inside its mouth, wrestles it to the surface, and slings it ashore. Not exactly the most beautiful piece of angling you'll see, nevertheless effective. An Oklahoma man holds the world record for largest catfish caught hogging. He caught the eighty-five-pound flathead at Lake Tawakoni, Texas in 2017.

CHAPTER 20

Let Them Eat Corn

Each of you should give what you have decided in your heart to give,

    not reluctantly or under compulsion, for God loves a cheerful giver.

2 Corinthians 9:7

Every bit of evidence points to the idea that it's hereditary, an instinct passed down through the generations over which there is no control. Certain conditions come together, maybe a freshness in the morning air, perhaps a blue bird that flutters by in the first promise of spring, and it sparks the familiar feeling. Country folks are drawn to the dirt. We have an innate call to put seeds in the ground, tend them, watch over them, and work with the earth to create something new.

When I planted my first garden with the remnants of vegetable seeds left over from the season's planting of the big garden my mom and dad raised that year, it meant several days clearing a thin blackberry thicket between two wild pecan trees near our home. But that was part of the adventure. There were two varieties of squash, some okra, and a little watermelon just for me. It was an amazingly satisfying, unprompted exercise, even for an eight-year-old boy who'd been around gardens all his young life. But this one was mine. I was the caretaker. The little patch would produce, or it would fail. Either way, it would be at my hand.

A city boy for decades now, I still raise a respectable back yard garden. There is something about the annual ritual of tilling the dirt, planting the seeds, and watching them grow, that compliments the idea of renewal, second chances, and fresh starts.

You'd be surprised how much pleasure there is in taking a walk out to the back yard just watching the garden's progress from one day to the next. It's no fewer than a ten-time-a-day ritual for me every day between March and July, oftentimes a nice break in my morning writing routine. I go out and just look, and it makes me happy, sort of a natural brain reset. A few moments of watching a bumble bee on a squash bloom can actually inspire.

We enjoy the fresh produce, but it all comes about so quickly there is always more than Dana and I can eat, and sharing it with others is a special joy.

In the midst of composing a social media post that offered free squash and lettuce to all our friends across town, I was reminded where all those instincts originate. It's true that sharing our garden produce seems as natural as the instinct of planting the garden itself.

I can vividly remember, and understand why.

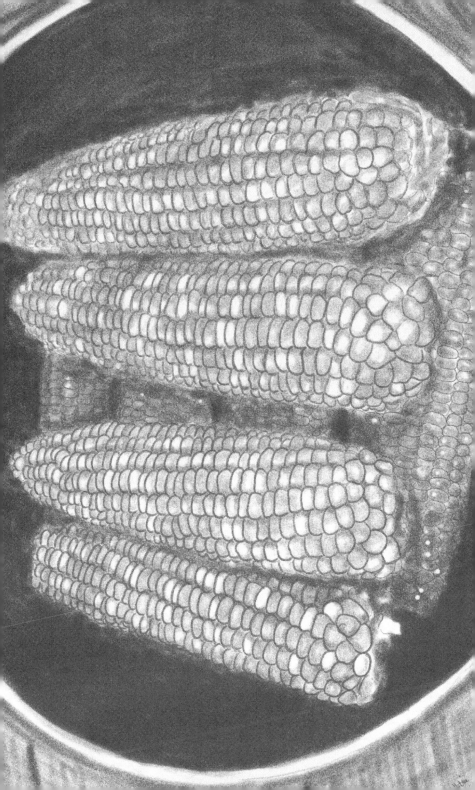

A generous spirit in a man can offset a lot of his less charming qualities. While he wasn't the most cash-rich man in the country, the king of Highbanks Road loved growing, and giving away good food.

There was never a year when my parents didn't raise a garden of at least a half acre. It oftentimes seemed a higher priority and produced more drama than the eight hundred acres of cotton we ultimately raised annually. It was amazing, really, how Dad compartmentalized a hard day's work on the farm, then dedicated his lunch hour or early evening hours before supper to caretaking in the garden. Everything about it was contrary to his outward personality. But there was an inner-satisfaction he derived from his garden tending.

There is a certain feeling we get as we display acts of kindness toward those who can never repay us. In the Bible, the gospel of Luke mentions this idea in chapter 14, recounting the story where Jesus dines with a prominent Pharisee and notices how several people took seats at places of honor around the table. Then he shared this parable:

> *When someone invites you to a wedding feast, do not take the place of honor, for a person more distinguished than you may have been invited ... For all who exalt themselves will be humbled, and those who humble themselves will be exalted. Then Jesus said to his host, When you give a luncheon or dinner, do not invite your friends, your brothers or sisters, your relatives or your rich neighbors. If you do, they may invite you back and so you will be repaid. But when you give a banquet, invite the poor, the crippled, the lame, the blind, and you will be blessed. Although they*

cannot repay you, you will be repaid at the resurrection of the righteous.

Luke 14:8-24

There were never any worldly or high spiritual motives in Dad's garden generosity. Maybe it was an unrecognized obedience to a call to serve that he never discerned. Or maybe it just made him happy.

When a large garden begins bearing fruit, it quickly becomes more of a daily job than most people intend. Tomatoes, cucumbers, okra, beans of all kind must be picked at the peak of their maturity, else they'll become tough, or rot on the vine. It's also a best practice that allows the plant to direct its energy to the new fruit. That means another picking tomorrow or the next day. After all the work of careful tending, protecting from late freeze, and watching for disease and insects through late spring, June and July are a non-stop daily harvest.

There were no cute baskets or decorative containers used in our garden harvest. The exponential volume inspired Dad to save five-gallon hydraulic fluid buckets that were far more practical than pretty. When you have thirty tomato plants, a fifty-yard row of purple hull peas, or three different varieties of squash and cucumbers, it doesn't take long to fill up enough buckets to take up the better part of a pickup truck bed. Early most mornings after picking through the humidity and the dew, and after he and Mom selected what they needed for the day, Dad would head for town leaving full buckets all around. All his loafing spots. The bank. The local coffee shop. Nursing homes. He did it long enough the message was implied. *Take whatever you like, just use what you take.* Over the years, there must have been hundreds who enjoyed the fruits of his labor.

One summer experiment when I was still off to college went a long way toward revealing Dad's nature as a garden giver. He'd become productive enough that he decided to dedicate a one-acre plot to a commercial sweet corn project. If you've never had freshly picked, fresh-boiled, peaches-and-cream variety sweet corn on the cob served alongside fried okra, black-eyed peas, corn-bread and cold-sliced tomatoes, you've not lived a full life. Dad and Mom invested countless hours and several gallons of sweat that spring tending and harvesting a bumper crop of corn for his stand on Highbanks Road. The corn produced almost faster than he could pick and sell it.

And selling it was a problem. Not that local folks weren't willing to pay their fair share for the seasonal delight. If it was someone Dad knew, he just couldn't force himself to take their money. "Put that money away. I'm not taking that." I saw him say it a hundred times. Somewhere along the way, a code of honor about giving away food made its way to a man who otherwise loved taking care of himself. When he gave, he gave by the bucket.

It wasn't the only pleasure Dad found on our little kingdom's acre-and-a-half home place.

There was another, one of his greatest pleasures, that nearly killed him.

CHAPTER 21

Purple Birds &
The Performance Gospel

The grace of God means something like: Here is your life.
You might never have been, but you are because the party
wouldn't have been complete without you.

Frederick Buechner

I'd heard him put a string of expletives together a thousand times, but this one was different. There was an angry sadness in his tone. You could sense defeat, something so unexpectedly bad that it could not be undone.

The summertime lunches the three of us spent together were the best times our family shared. Mom was on summer vacation from teaching, but always the piddler, stayed busy doing her share in the garden, canning, preserving, and assembling a hot lunch at straight-up noon. For years in my early teens, we sat together as family at a little three-person kitchen bar talking about the day and enjoying freshly cooked garden fare, usually with a side of fried cornbread, and tea so ridiculously sweet that it poured thick as honey. After lunch, we'd take a thirty-minute nap, me on the couch and Dad in his reclining chair, before heading back for a long afternoon of tractor duty. It happened one lunch hour when Dad skipped his nap for some outside garden chores. The tone of his voice jolted me from deep sleep.

Over the years, Dad had developed an uncharacteristic love for bird watching. His interest in watching them in the yard was just as strong hunting them along the fencerow or on the river. And he'd become particularly fond of a family of barn swallows that returned to our open carport each year where they nested on a corner ledge. It was a perfect spot for watching the male and female over several months as they built a mud-daubed nest, incubated the eggs, hatched them, fed and protected the young, and eventually bid goodbye as the young birds fledged and started new families. Watching those birds became daily summer conversation, and a family tradition that we all loved.

It was early July and the year's four fledglings were already standing tall and stretching their wings, days from independence and flight.

Just as Dad walked from the garden back to the carport, he heard a strange commotion, and something totally out of the ordinary caught the corner of his eye. He did a double-take comprehending the reality.

A seven-foot, jet black, king snake had wrapped itself around a white metal column, slowing inching its way up toward the nest. Jaws unhinged, one by one, he gorged himself on the fledglings as the adult swallows flogged the snake, unaffected by their helpless, chaotic panic. By the time he could run for a hoe, the last bird was devoured, and the snake slithered downward, mission accomplished.

With the razor-sharp end of the hoe, Dad pulled the snake from the column, slicing head from body with one quick blow. *Maybe, there's time,* he thought, and taking an old pocketknife he ripped he snake's throat and belly open only to discover it was too late. The reptile's constrictive muscles had already squeezed life from the young fledglings, now limp. He sat helplessly on the ground, knife in hand, and blood up to his elbows, the dead reptile's nervous system still causing its severed body to wriggle and jerk along the ground a bit. He'd never appeared more defeated, or completely powerless. I walked toward him timidly, and speechless, in a surreal scene — a fifty-year-old man with an open knife staring off into nowhere as sad as a child. He would hardly look up before the words finally came.

"I hope he was hungry. That's the last meal that son of a bitch will ever eat."

It wasn't long following that incident that Dad got more proactive in the birdwatching business. When he learned our home location was central to the migratory path of the purple martin, he went all-in as a host to hundreds of birds. There was something about this delicate bird, its lovely soaring flight patterns, and its practical purpose for eating hundreds of mosquitos each day, that he simply loved. But mostly, as weird as it may sound, I think preparing the housing and the perfect environment made him feel fatherly in some ways.

Each January, the purple martin begins its nesting migration from the tropical climates of central America and Mexico toward the mainland United States and as far as southern Canada. They are more dependent upon man-made housing for nesting than just about any other bird, and prefer living in communities where birders provide white, gourd-like commercial housing in a season that lasts February through July when the young martins fledge and begin their return southward.

Maintaining between fifty and seventy-five houses just across the Highbanks Road drainage ditch each year, Dad sat in a lawn chair, happy as could be, BB gun or .22 caliber rifle in hand warding off hungry or bothersome prey. He was the landlord to a flock of hundreds of the sweet-chirping acrobats that entertained him with their swooping and gliding for hours. In his late sixties, he even learned how to use the internet so he could track the migration when it began, and watched again in the fall to see the birds home. Loafing buddies called him Bird Man.

After her retirement from forty-three years in public schools, Mom bought a second house in the town where I live. She wanted to be closer to me, and her grandchildren, and she needed some independence from a relationship where she'd always been the adult. No one ever called it a separation, but that's exactly what it was. Dad would eventually move, and the old home farmhouse would get sold whenever he was good and ready. Their separate lives went on for more than a year, until one day, Mom realized nobody had heard from him in three days. An uncle drove to the farm to check on him the next morning.

As he pulled into the driveway everything appeared normal. Dad's truck was parked in its regular spot and everything seemed intact. The door was unlocked, so he announced himself loudly, and walked in, unprepared for the immediate sight.

Dad was sitting cross-legged, naked on the kitchen floor rocking back and forth like a child, feces and urine all around. He was conscious, but unresponsive with an empty look in his eyes. How long he'd been that way is still a mystery.

When the ambulance arrived, the driver and emergency medical technician quickly learned something that a few of us already knew. David Watkins was as strong as a bull, and virtually impossible to control when he wished not to be controlled. What they discovered was a man strangely out of his senses, oblivious even to his own need for help. He swung violent, but completely uncontrolled, haymaking fists at the EMTs, as if to protect himself from harm.

It required all three men and a shot of morphine to wrestle him into the ambulance and strap him down for the forty-minute ride to the hospital. He cussed each one like a bird dog. Ambulance workers later said they'd never had a more violent passenger. Even with maximum restraint, Dad kicked a hole in the roof with his bare feet. Eventually, the sedatives brought rest.

When I arrived at the hospital emergency room, his voice echoed loudly through the halls, swearing violently at the medical team trying to assess the circumstances. It was like a hurricane in the small examination room, and a scenario far too serious for embarrassment.

For the next week, Mom and I lived in a critical care hospital unit, consulting with neurologists, infectious disease, and internal medicine specialists, each of whom was confounded by Dad's complete lack of responsiveness to any stimulation or treatment. No longer the violent man they'd admitted, Dad, except for his breathing, appeared lifeless. After ten days we considered the reality that none of our lives might ever be the same.

Then, on the thirteenth day in the late afternoon, he stirred to life.

"I sure am hungry," he rolled slowly to the bedside looking at Mom through glassy eyes. "And I feel terrible. Where the hell am I?" His awakening was contrary to everything we'd begun to believe about the future. Just how far he'd return to us was still a mystery.

But each day, progress.

As his communication became clearer, doctors assigned a diagnosis of viral meningitis, likely contracted from cleaning his purple martin housing in the off season. It would have killed a weaker man, they all agreed. He simply refused to die. But the reality of how close he actually came wasn't lost on him.

In his final days of that hospital stay, he approached a transparent conversation with me one afternoon. "The good Lord sure did spare me. I don't know why, but He did. I believe it's time I started living a different kind of life," he said. "Well, all of us can always do better than we're doing," I said hopefully. It was the beginning of another short window of opportunity when his weakness trumped his desire, and my lingering resentment got in the way of everything that was noble. We should have talked more about that different life right there. Truth is, I'd heard talk like this a dozen times before, but never saw any real effort to make it happen.

This was our history. Both of us, genuinely in our hearts, wanted to do better toward the other, and yet we consistently failed.

Why is it that we all have such a difficult time living out a life that we know is honorable? Our desires are authentic. Our intentions good and pure. And yet we painfully miss the mark. It's almost as if some powerful barrier exists between our actions and the very thing we claim as our heart's desire.

The apostle Paul had something profound and hopeful to say about situations like this in Romans 7 and 8. It resonates at the heart of the simple gospel message that Dad had so much difficulty retaining, and the void he experienced when trying to understand his own self-worth. It is a beautiful answer to the question of this inner struggle, and an amazing picture of God's lavish grace.

> *So I find this law at work: Although I want to do good, evil is right there with me. For in my inner being I delight in God's law; but I see another law at work in me, waging war against the law of my mind and making me a prisoner of the law of sin at work within me. What a wretched man I am! Who will rescue me from this body that is subject to death?*
> *Romans 7:21-24*

What does Paul see when he looks in the mirror?

He sees a person who wants to produce Kingdom fruit, a person who wants to grow in Christ because he knows this is the Way, but when he looks at himself in the eyes of the law, sin's dominion over him is only strengthened. He can never measure up, and sees a reflection depicting a forever-failure against the mirror of law.

Verse 25 sets the stage for a revelation in Romans 8 of the best news we can know, and the most important news we can share at home and abroad.

Thanks be to God, who delivers me through Jesus Christ our Lord!

And then the freedom made forever true when Jesus gave up his spirit on the cross.

> *Therefore, there is now no condemnation for those who are in Christ Jesus, because through Christ Jesus the law of the Spirit who gives life has set you free from the law of sin and death. For what the law was powerless to do because it was weakened by the flesh, God did by sending his own Son in the likeness of sinful flesh to be a sin offering. And so he condemned sin in the flesh, in order that the righteous requirement of the law might be fully met in us, who do not live according to the flesh but according to the Spirit.*
>
> *Romans 8:1-4*

No condemnation.

That is the good news of the gospel.

There is no condemnation.

Why didn't I share those words with Dad so many years before?

Chapter 22

The Hog Lady

*Just think how happy you would be if you lost everything
you have right now, then got it back again.*

Frances Rodman

Everyone called her the Hog Lady.

And if there was an arch nemesis in my father's uncomplicated
life, she was it.

In the 1970s and 80s, most small cotton farms were anywhere
from eighty to five hundred acres. Oftentimes, the family rented
another four or five hundred acres from landowners no longer
actively engaged on the farm. Some such folks were retired couples.
Many were widows. These land-rent arrangements typically allow
the landowner one-third of the farm revenue, while the farmer
takes two-thirds. It is generally a simple and mutually-beneficial
arrangement without much hassle for either party.

But it can also be the worst of nagging thorns in a farmer's side when the personalities just don't jibe.

As my dad's farming operation grew toward eight hundred acres, he had the opportunity around 1984 to rent eighty acres from Maureen Chambliss, a local widow who had a side hustle raising hogs.

Her home place comprised a simple two-bedroom brick home, barn, fencing, feeding troughs, all the kinds of things you'd imagine. But there were no barriers between the pigs and the house. They were free to run wild through her home place, and did so daily. This was a situation so strange for all the countryside residents that no one ever questioned it. You just drove by, and kept driving.

Maureen wore tall rubber boots everywhere she went. She was loud, could cuss better than anyone, and was one of the most demanding landlords you'd ever find. The price for farming her land meant you also created a nice garden spot for her, took her to the grocery store or hoped that someone in your family would if you were busy, and helped her make her doctor appointments, among so many other things. She thought her land was better and more productive than anyone else's, and she'd use this leverage to take advantage of guys like my dad who needed the land and the income. Landowners can wield a certain power over a farmer who needs the money. These relationships become a powder keg over time.

Maureen's steady pressure on Dad was so great that he reluctantly turned down a two-week trip to Europe with my mom one summer, and on one of the rare occasions when they could make the trip together. He feared his absence would set her off so much that she'd take the land the following year. Imagine a puppet master dangling a performing marionette. That was the essence of their relationship.

Dad and Maureen had some volatile times. It all ended one day when she called him to fix a water pump and they got crossways and into a cussing fight over something crop related. I wish I could have seen the two going at it. My mind paints a picture as she lorded over him, cussing a blue streak in those rubber boots.

He always regretted not taking that trip to Europe. And he was a man much more at peace when that caustic relationship ended and he was no longer beholden to the Hog Lady.

But he was also a man who could self-destruct his own peace in a heartbeat.

CHAPTER 23

Jail Talk

Blessed is the man who, having nothing to say, abstains from giving us wordy evidence of the fact.

George Eliot

A twelve-year-old boy is fragile cargo. He's trying to figure out a dozen things about himself while the hormones rage, and he's hypersensitive to all the external forces pointing him in multiple directions, most of them the wrong. No longer a boy, not yet a man, he is malleable to all potential influences, and destined to become all that he allows through the filter of his senses and young judgment.

At this tender age, he begins making choices, not only consequential, but eternal.

There must have been a dozen potential responses running through my young mind when he declared it from nowhere.

"You sure don't talk very much," he said, beer between legs and cigarette in hand as we fulfilled his favorite Saturday afternoon pastime, driving dirt roads from the state line package store along the river toward home.

Are you kidding me? You never even talk with me. You just talk at me. And you're drunk more than half the time. What is it you want me to talk about? How scared I'll be when we walk in the door wondering just how much you'll lie to Mom about how much you've had to drink?

"I guess I'm just a quiet person," my official response, simultaneously avoiding conflict and sensing my father's own disappointment in our relationship. *Is this my fault?* It felt like walking under a cloud of guilt.

If there is one valuable lesson for learning in life, it's this:

When you don't know what to say, keep your mouth shut.

When you're uncertain of the wisdom in what you're about to speak, zip your lips.

And if it seems like a good moment when the other person in the conversation needs to think on what she's just said, shut your pie hole.

There is a world of hurt that comes from a careless thought spoken too quickly, and there's no harm in the silence.

It's a lesson that came in handy managing one of the most unexpected situations in my adult life.

Thirty years later, married with children, it was helpful recalling our brief pickup truck exchange after taking a phone call early one Saturday evening. It was one of my dad's "hired hands," a full-time employee on our farm, with the last kind of news you ever expect.

"Steve, your dad's in the county jail and you need to go get him," the voice at the other end said.

"What?"

It was a common response to occasional bewildering news about my dad.

"Your dad. He's in jail. But if you'll go get him, they'll let him out."

By my early forties, I'd experienced many odd things Dad-related. I'd seen him escape two near-death experiences. He'd lied about once being so drunk he couldn't find his way home on a Saturday afternoon when there were tornados all around. He even went on a whiskey bender one day, getting so drunk he rode a horse bareback until his inner thighs became so raw that he bled for days. But never did I expect a phone call with instructions like this.

"Why is my dad in jail?" I was surprised at my own presence of mind to even ask.

"He got in a fight with the new town cop. I seen the whole thing," he said. "They pulled him over for speeding and he didn't want to cooperate. Next thing you knew he was handcuffed, belly-down on the ground."

Suddenly, it all made perfect sense.

Once in a while, rural police departments will take on an outsider — a new employee unfamiliar with local people and local ways, who has a need to prove himself. It's just the kind of attitude David Watkins despised in a man. But nine times out of ten, a young buck fresh out of police academy can do just exactly what the rookie did to my older and overweight father. He was in the back of a cop car headed for jail before he knew what happened.

Yes. Constructing the scene in my mind, it made sense. Even if it was an over-the-top reaction on the cop's part.

Suddenly, it was like a reverse transport in time. All I could see was that twelve-year-old boy in a smoke-filled pickup truck getting placed in a terribly awkward position, not knowing what to do or say next. The irresolution of my childhood flooded every sense.

How do I even do this?

It was only a twenty-minute drive to the jail. But I'd pick Dad up, then have a long, forty-mile drive back to the old hometown where the cops had stored his truck. We'd have at least an hour together alone. And this might easily be the most pivotal moment in our relationship. I could only imagine his mood and frame of mind. His spirit would be wounded and that made my dad extremely unpredictable. The moment called for only one possible undertone — dutiful son, and complete absence from judgment. *Just do the job, and let him do the talking.*

There's a long winding driveway that leads to the county jail off Highway 63B. It makes its way around security fences topped with razor wire and past a large garden plot where prisoners raise their own fresh food during summer and fall. It was nearly sunset, and a dozen prisoners clad in white jumpsuits were cutting okra in the cool of the day. Mourning doves cooed, and cicadas were well into their evening song. A perfectly normal night in the South, *except ...*

Walking toward the entrance I could see a security door and a speaker about head high. Before buzzing me in, they were going to ask my identification and why I was there.

What am I supposed to say? I'm here to pick up a prisoner? Someone told me my dad's in jail? I could feel my heart rate accelerating.

On cue to pushing the button, an authoritative voice responded. "Can I help you, sir?"

"I'm here to pick up David Watkins."

There was maybe a thirty-second delay.

"Come on in and have a seat. We'll have him out to you in just a moment."

The steel door buzzed and clicked, and I walked into the jailhouse. That first minute seemed surprisingly uncomplicated.

The sitting room was nicer than expected. Dark blue carpet and light-blue painted cinder-block walls. Probably on purpose as a soothing color combination. There were three small windows beyond the security glass where the officer on duty sat, and you could see the cage-like auditorium just beyond. Twenty minutes passed. Then a large iron door clicked open and slammed hard shut so that it echoed throughout. It was the perfect jailhouse cliché. In a secluded security room two officers returned Dad's personal effects. He was calm, but his body language was that of a man ready to be somewhere else.

He walked out, purposely straight toward me, eyes down.

"Get me the hell out of here."

I pointed him toward my truck's direction, not speaking yet.

As we exited the building, he exhaled a ton of tension. I asked if he was okay. "Yes, I think I'm fine," he said.

"That son of a bitch had me on the ground before I knew what happened," Dad said. "I didn't even do anything. He'll get his turn." It was moments like this when right, or wrong, the man's temper erased all lines of authority and rule.

Remember, just listen. No judgment.

"I just want to make sure you're okay," I said.

"Yes, I'm okay, just a little bunged up." I could see the scratches on his forearms where he'd been wrestled to the pavement.

In this most awkward circumstance, we were actually having a civil and productive conversation. During the next few quiet moments, I could see him running the entire scene through his head, over and over. Not about the rightness or wrongness. More likely about how he could have done a few things differently and whipped the young cop. He'd had those same regrets for not beating Elmer Duncan with a crescent wrench.

Never had I felt like such an adult in my father's presence. Showing the outer disgust of picking my dad up at the county jail on a Saturday night would have been easy. Moreover, it would have been a vindictive payback for all the times I felt berated as young boy. But there was nothing that felt right about acting that way. Not one thing.

Entering town and turning north toward the old home place where Mom and Dad still farmed, we were there in minutes. It was almost enough secret pleasure that Mom had heard the news and was waiting. He thanked me for the trouble, and I couldn't resist a parting shot that I hoped he'd take the right way.

"I don't ever want to have to do this again," I said in a stern, parental tone.

Luckily, he laughed a little. Then we both belly-laughed together.

The embarrassment only cost him about a month's absence from the local coffee shop. The bad thing about living in a small town is that everyone knows everything.

Oftentimes country folk know your dirty laundry long before it spreads through the family. That's exactly what happened in a winter incident soon after, which drove a wedge between my father and me for fifteen years.

Chapter 24

The Last Lie

Temporary, but excruciating, pain is the price of healing.
Vironika Tugaleva

In small communities, everyone knows the really bad personal stuff long before you. That's what amplifies the hurt and embarrassment so much, once you come to the knowledge. You see clearly, that in retrospect, every sign was there, and you were likely blinded by hope.

When Mom called with the news, there was an immediate flashback to a moment eighteen months earlier that was odd enough to capture my attention, but not so much that I spent any time investigating or thinking on it further.

I was almost a year into my first job working as a copy editor at *Florida Today* in Melbourne, Florida, where I learned both quickly, and surprisingly enough after all the years of just wanting to leave, that I missed something about the Southern way of life.

The longing for home messed up every career plan I'd make for the next twenty years. But after ten months away, it was powerful enough that having no picture of the future was okay. Dad flew on a one-way ticket to Florida where we'd pack up the apartment, do a quick turnaround, and he'd take the lead driving a U-Haul a thousand miles homeward over two days. From there, everything was a blank sheet.

That evening during a break in the packing he asked a strange question.

"Where can I find a pay phone?"

"Around the corner by the 7-Eleven, but the landline is still good," I said. "Use it."

"No, I need a pay phone. I'll be back in twenty minutes." I tried again, but he was insistent. All the possible circumstances ran through my mind for a moment, but with a Category 1 hurricane on the way, expected to make landfall right about the time we'd depart, the distractions came easily. I just wanted to pack and go home.

For the next eighteen months, my parents — now empty nesters for nearly three years — experienced a disconnect that would shape us all for the next decade.

David Watkins was many things. He lied about his drinking. He lied covering up important financial matters about the farm. He had an explosive temper. But strange as it sounds, I never thought of him as a mean, or even a deceitful person. Truth is, he was a lot like a handful of other men in the community. He wasn't the greatest behavior model, but he could have been much worse.

But there was a different kind of void that surfaced in their relationship creating an emptiness for both, the kind of emptiness that will cause a weak-minded man to look for ways to fill it.

It was just two weeks before Christmas when my mom called. Her tone was unusually disquieting.

"He has a girlfriend."

"What?"

"Your dad. He has a girlfriend now. Apparently, he wasn't even hiding it any longer, because everyone in the country knew but me. I feel so stupid," and she began crying.

A concerned family member had finally seen enough that she called Mom and gave her the news. She found him not long afterward at his favorite drinking joint, the woman by his side. As she opened the door, their eyes met and a long lie suddenly ended. Drunk out of his mind, he was surprisingly calm. With a single motion of his arm, and a belligerent, beer-numbed look on his face, he destroyed her.

"Go on, and get out of here," he slurred.

"That's what you want?" she asked.

"Go on."

He didn't come home for weeks, and when he did, the reality of just how broken their relationship had become was all the more evident.

Farm families are not made up of individuals. The unit is a team and all things are tied together, not the least of which is its financial structure. My mom's stable income as a public school teacher, and our land, had for years been the single financial pillar that allowed Dad to literally risk the farm annually. After a two-week stretch away from home prowling the countryside like a drunken tomcat, he sat on the couch, face in his palms with a confession that only made the wounds deeper.

"I have to come home," he said.

"Why is that?" Mom asked.

"The bank will never loan crop money if I'm not here."

The wounds never completely healed. For years there was an annual cycle when my parents would have a major falling out in the weeks prior to Christmas. There's nothing enjoyable about sitting down to Christmas dinner when you can see the anger in one parent's eyes, and the hurt in the other's. Forgiveness is always the right thing. Rarely is it the easy thing.

For me, Dad had drawn a line in the sand that I mistakenly believed forced me to choose a side. Given that scenario, everyone knew my choice. I had a loyalty to Mom, who I always knew was the compassionate leader. That he betrayed her in such a way stirred up a lingering hate inside me. Until the final weeks leading up to his death, our relationship, not great from the beginning, was never the same. If only I'd known how many of his failures and shortcomings I'd repeat in my own life.

Time brings understanding. It's just a shame how much the healing can hurt everyone.

CHAPTER 25

Judge Not ...

The man who passes judgment should also swing the sword.
George R.R. Martin

Somebody's gonna get hurt and you're going to be the one who does it.
  The hospital psychiatrist's words echoed a reality that had never been more real, prompting the first uncertain steps of passage through a relationship hurricane that destroyed nearly everyone in its path. So many moments, I thought my death would have been the easiest escape for everyone involved. That I had put myself in the position of such moral failure was not only unfathomable, it was the ultimate irony — the thing for which I'd despised my father most.

The thing a commanding, domineering, control-obsessed parent will do to you the most is put you in a hurry. You are in a hurry to leave the room, try to make the day end quickly. Get on to the next thing. You dream of that day when you leave them, free and on your own, once and forever, no more rules. What it most did for me was to rush me into relationships that I believed helped escape his belittlement. From the time of young childhood, I was dreaming about a wife and a new home where he had no say, and where there would be no thought about him, or need for him. There wasn't a night that went by for fifteen years when I didn't dream that dream. From junior high to college, I never looked for a girlfriend. I sought out a wife.

From about fourteen on, what time I didn't spend on the farm or the basketball court I spent with a girl. Girlfriends were like emotional salve, and time with them was different than hanging out with my male friends. It filled a void that prompted acceptance and love. It was probably no coincidence that my longtime high school girlfriend was also the cheerleading captain. Those early relationships usually lasted several months to a year or more, mostly because I clung to them. As each one ended, I also began understanding something new about myself — I would crawl under a rock to avoid an argument or the slightest conflict. It was probably the worst attribute I brought to a nineteen-year marriage in 1988.

The first three years of college were different. Still holding the purse strings, my father had imposed restrictions that limited traditional social life at a university. There were no fraternity parties, he prohibited ROTC and other group affiliations, and summers were still for work back home on the farm. There were very few dates, and no girlfriends. Then something interesting happened my junior year.

Working as news editor of the college newspaper, I received dozens of stories from undergraduates who submitted their work for weekly publication. One name that came across the desk frequently showed extraordinary promise as a young writer. That was the first thing that piqued my interest, and for a while, I just watched.

First semester of my senior near, now working as editor-at-large, I asked that young woman to serve on staff as news editor. I did everything I could to get to know her through a guarded personality that intrigued me all the more.

Never more than at this point was I in an unnecessary hurry.

As spring break rolled around several months into our dating, our graduation date loomed. It seemed like some future moment when anything and everything suddenly became uncertain, and I hated uncertainty. If there was one thing I'd promised myself upon leaving home, it was stability, predictability, and routine — all of which I'd never experienced, but desperately desired. The thought of future loneliness and a complete blank slate terrified me. So, on the return leg of a flight from spring break in Florida, I proposed marriage to the young woman I'd pursued for a year, and actually courted for a few months. She said yes. In retrospect, I believe she felt many of the same things I was feeling - that marriage was simply the next thing. Four months later on a steaming hot July day, we were married. The air conditioning failed in the church that day and everyone was miserable. Maybe it was a warning sign.

The first fifteen years of that marriage were predictable enough. Three remarkable children were born. We worked our way into the community as respectable journalists before I pursued careers in public service and higher education, while she launched a family magazine business with me and an old college friend as silent partners. The business caught fire, I left a stable, high-paying job in higher education to manage our sales, and even with three children we found ourselves suddenly making more money than we could spend. It looked picture perfect even to our closest friends. But relationally, we'd both become empty vessels.

A conflict avoider who feels lonely in a long-term relationship will do two things.

First, over time he will pour himself into different situations where he may experience some sense of success and validation.

My fundraising team during a career at Arkansas State University raised $7 million a year. My sales team at the magazine approached $1 million in sales our second year. I began running, and the short distances weren't enough, so I began training for a full marathon, ran three in eighteen months, and lost eighty-five pounds in the process. My yard and garden were pristine, the envy of the neighborhood. I became deeply involved in church, taught Sunday School, and for nearly two years led an hour-long men's class each Wednesday beginning at 6 A M — this also becoming a great irony.

Behind closed doors at home, we shared a brother-sister relationship at best. She quietly resented my pursuits of distraction. I was resolute to the idea that she had no real love for me, and so I bottled up in silence. All the warning signs were there. It was a Friday afternoon dispute in 2006 that first prompted the idea of how seriously we were in trouble.

After missing the finishing-time goal in my first marathon by a substantial margin in December 2005, I immediately began training for the next opportunity, Nashville's Country Music Marathon, another four months down the road. The training regimen took no prisoners. I was running fifty-four miles over three days every week, and weight training another two. From a peak weight of two hundred forty pounds, I was now at a sleek one sixty-five. I'd done everything a person needed to do to complete the twenty-six miles in four hours and twenty minutes. Obsessive compulsion is a great companion when you're lonely.

Packing for the four-hour drive to Nashville that Friday around noon, my phone rang and my wife was in a panic. There'd been a software breakdown at the office and she was having difficulty making a publication deadline. With a race check-in time that loomed three hundred miles down the road and after four months of complete dedication to a cause, she wanted me to come to work knowing I'd miss the event. The telephone argument lasted almost an hour. In a rare and uncharacteristic moment of rebellion, I finished packing and headed for Nashville. She genuinely needed some help. In the moment, I thought it the most selfish request imaginable. Thinking about the conflict, I became so sick during the race that I walked off at the halfway mark and drove home. Hours later, with our kids in the same room, she looked me in the eye and said it was the closest she'd ever come to leaving me. I hated being made the bad guy in front of the kids, in whose lives I'd been equal partner at least.

It was the first time in our relationship words like that were spoken aloud. I wasn't so angry as empty. It's likely she felt the same. From that moment, our marriage disintegrated, slowly at first, then picking up speed just a year later.

The second thing a conflict avoider will do over time is exhibit the slow boil of a pressure cooker. Conflict avoiders are all-or-nothing, black-or-white partners in a relationship. We need the peace that comes with complete security and happiness, the irony being that all the while we won't work through the inevitable contention that comes in a relationship. When a conflict avoider hits slow boil, it only takes the slightest misspoken word or careless deed to trigger a meltdown. Later that year and just before Christmas, I could no longer stand the anticipated pleasure of gifting a new smartphone I'd chosen for her, so I gave it to her at work one day. She reacted mostly with with what I perceived as anger for a reason I never understood. Most likely I'd done something else to cause frustration, but that moment, a switch flipped somewhere inside me. Or maybe at that point I was just looking for an excuse.

I'd fired Dana Hoggard in a previous fundraising career at Arkansas State nearly two years earlier because my boss insisted she be let go. I carried out the termination thinking it was a raw deal, and hired Dana to work in sales for me at the magazine when I took over there. She was much better at selling advertising than philanthropy, and she had a personality that helped bring a sales team together. We'd never been more than distant friends, but were now killing it together as a sales team.

She was divorced. I was lonely, except for the fulfillment that went with watching three young children grow, thrive, and excel. One day, just as I was staring through my office window watching the snow begin to fall, Dana brought me a cup of hot chocolate. It felt like the nicest thing anyone had done for me in years, and I thought about the small, but kind gesture for days.

I became interested in knowing more about Dana, so I found reasons for more meetings, strategy sessions, and even the occasional joint sales call. We were both in vulnerable places, and for the entire next January, I couldn't stop thinking about her. The all-or-nothing gene was moving in a different direction. Late one Sunday afternoon, I sent Dana a text asking to meet with her at work early the next morning. She agreed. It's the only night I've never slept a single wink.

She was on time the next morning at 7, came in, and I closed the door almost unable to speak the words I'd rehearsed all night. I'd been in a completely faithful relationship for almost nineteen years and was about to do the unthinkable by breaking that trust.

Trying to prevent the hyperventilation I spit it out.

"Is there something going on between us we're not talking about?"

Her face was expressionless, and there was a long pause, like time left the room.

"Well, I don't think so, but even if there was, I don't know much we could do about it," she acknowledged the reality.

"That's true enough," I replied, feeling both relief and sadness at the same time.

We talked for another forty-five minutes until other staffers started arriving, and it seemed she took on the role of counselor more than the object of my attention. I read situations for a living, and had no idea what to make of this one. For the first time in nineteen years, I felt like an unfaithful husband as she walked out the door. What's more, I could feel my all-or-nothing personality tilting like the uneven weight on a scale. My upbringing and religious belief meant divorce had never been a real option on the table, though at times I'd actually prayed that God would take me so I'd be free from that marriage. Anyone who prays that prayer is not well. There were no options to freedom that would not devastate my children.

Two hours later, Dana called and asked if I'd be interested in lunch to talk some more. Of course I was. Two weeks later, we sat across the desk from one another once again and I told her I was going to marry her. We hadn't even held hands. Switch flipped and still in a hurry after all these years. Right or wrong, some things will never change for a conflict-avoider embroiled in relationship.

There is no good time to walk out on a nineteen-year relationship that involves young children. I'd become too hurt to consider any pain it might bring to my wife, but the kids were different. When they all returned from a Sunday drive that afternoon, I was gone. A month later, I handed her the divorce papers. The pain that it caused those kids for the following months and over the next several years lies squarely on my shoulders. I still pray for their undeserved forgiveness.

The year that followed was hell. A conflict avoider in the throes of divorce is the ultimate irony. Throw in collateral damage to important relationships and the violation of your own moral conscience, and it is a recipe for chronic depression. This, all further complicated by feeling loved for the first time in more than a decade.

I tried every way I knew to make divorce easy. Walked away from everything. Contested nothing. Gave up a flourishing business, half of which I'd built. Relinquished my home, paid off tens of thousands of dollars in credit card debt, and agreed to monthly support payments totaling nearly two hundred thousand dollars over the next thirteen years. There is no amount of money you can pay to make the hurt, guilt, and shame disappear, but you try not to think about it too much because of all the hurt you caused everyone else. It seems undeservingly self-centered mourning a loss that you mostly created.

In what seemed like another realm, I continued spending time with Dana before my wife and I were officially divorced, and so I was officially an adulterer. It is such an ugly word, and it causes a lot of pain. It was inconceivable that I now wore the label, but in that realm, someone loved me and I could feel it, and it was my ambiguous saving grace. All I'd ever wanted, really.

Dana stood squarely by my side through the three years of chronic depression that followed, never once wavering. I was out of a job during the recession, almost unemployable, and there were many months we didn't know how the groceries would get bought. It seemed the healing would never come.

The ultimate irony is that I'd now become that thing for which I hated my father most, and taken it a step further. He never once threw it in my face, which was one of the most gracious gestures he ever made toward me.

CHAPTER 26

Her Majesty

She has fought many wars, most internal. The ones that you battle alone.

For this, she is remarkable. She is a survivor.

Nikki Rowe

It's funny how our regional culture is one where many people still think about distinguished Southern gentlemen with impeccable moral standards leading families and carrying on traditions like escorting young daughters to debutante balls. The stereotype makes a nice story but almost never applies. For two generations it was my gracious, generous, and wisdom-filled mother, not some stately man in a seersucker suit and white bucks, who was the undisputed head of the family.

Of all the elements that go into creating an interesting story, the experts say there are two critical points of view. You *feel* the story through the eyes of the protagonist. The villain escalates your blood pressure enough that he keeps you turning pages to the point of some acceptable resolution.

Neither protagonist or villain, Margaret Watkins is no less significant to this story. In fact, if not for her, there would be no story at all. It may not work this way in the Old Country, but without the queen, there would have been no king of Highbanks Road.

They were an unlikely pair. A blue-collar factory worker who loved to drag race and sew all kinds of wild oats, just thrilled to be away from his abusive father, and a promising graduate student following in her mother's footsteps with a career in education. They came together on a blind date. She said so many times how she initially viewed him as a good ol' country boy. He knew she was the catch of a lifetime, but he loved freedom. Two years passed and the factory worker avoided every possible commitment. That is, until the grad student offered an exasperated ultimatum one night that they would be married or go their separate ways. The very next day, there was a formal wedding, complete with dress, cake, and punch. Once Mom's mind was made up, all of hell's fury couldn't stand in her way.

I never had the chance to be anything other than my mama's greatest admirer. An only child gets all the attention, but her love was genuine and, most importantly, unconditional. With a father who took every opportunity to make you feel *less than*, Mom was the cheerleader every young man needs. The sheer volume of sweaty clothes she washed from thousands of basketball practices was amazing. I rarely remember waking up without the sound of a washing machine spinning across the house. She was royalty who served everyone before thought of self ever crossed her mind, and she exhibited a leadership style that always brought a prominent Bible story to mind. When it comes to all the ways we're wired to serve from the heart, there will be Marys, and there will be Marthas.

There are all kinds of leadership and hospitality styles in business and family. Nowhere are two styles better differentiated than in Luke, Chapter 10, where Jesus and his disciples pass through a village and receive a welcoming into the home of a woman named Martha, who had a sister called Mary. Both were ecstatic to welcome the special guests. They just honored the group differently.

It always feels like Martha gets a bad rap in this story.

Mary joins the group in a sitting room of sorts and reclines at Jesus' feet. What she most wants is to listen to Jesus. Mary, who probably most preferred the love language Dr. Gary Chapman describes today as quality time, wanted nothing more than a seat at the table. It was all about the present moment. This was the natural way she honored people.

Martha, on the other hand, was all about acts of service.

While Mary and the guests relaxed and conversed, Martha scurried about in a sweat, pots and pans banging with a hot fire roaring in the oven. Martha wanted to serve her very best, but her mistake in this instance was thinking Mary should be more like her. When she had enough, Martha asked Jesus what he thought about her sister's relaxed state of mind, as she literally slaved in a hot kitchen.

Jesus' rebuke was to the point, not for her efforts, but mostly because she wanted everyone doing things her way.

"Martha, Martha," the Lord answered, "you are worried and upset about many things, but few things are needed—or indeed only one. Mary has chosen what is better, and it will not be taken away from her."

It was not my impatient father, but a soft-spoken teacher of a mother who placed me behind the wheel of her Chevy Impala that summer of 1976 and gave a daily driving lesson along the gravel roads. I was ten years old. Whatever I learned from family, Mom was the teacher. Many years later in adulthood, it was Mom who I instinctively called several times daily during a chronic depression so deep I never thought I'd be myself again. When he's forty-five years old, sometimes a man still just needs to hear his mama's voice, even if he knows she doesn't have the answer.

In a world of Marys and Marthas, Mama was a Martha, though she served without judgment toward others. Her joy was fulfilled in service, her legacy the cornerstone that held everything together and kept the peace.

Sometimes, the real leader is the one standing back quietly in the distance.

Thank goodness she got at least one good one on my father that I'll never forget.

The couch in our family living room wasn't for formal social settings or tea parties or bridge gatherings. It was mostly the place where my father slept. Afternoon naps. Pre-supper naps. After-supper naps. Drunken, sleep-it-off naps. And that's usually where Dad, an intolerable snorer, slept until he decided to get up and go to bed sometime after midnight.

Mom was a professional woman, but she also enjoyed things that went into making our house a home. She regularly read a syndicated column in the Sunday paper called *Hints from Heloise*.

Heloise once suggested to a concerned reader who had problems with a snoring husband that she should spray a little perfume in near-proximity the moment he began sawing logs. Mom never forgot stuff like this.

Not long after Mom had read that particular piece of advice, Dad went into his Saturday night routine. Mom slipped back to the bedroom, self-satisfied with the problem she was about to remedy.

Two things went wrong: as Dad was snoring, Mom got *way* too close at the same moment Dad took an inhaling breath that was especially deep and long. He sucked every bit of the perfume mist into his lungs.

Indeed, the snoring stopped.

Coughing and gagging uncontrollably, he sat upright immediately unable to catch his breath. His nose bled profusely. He found the appropriate cuss words in between coughs and gags, but the blood was the worst part. We all thought she'd killed him. It took a day or so for that one to blow over. I'm not sure either of us felt terribly sorry for him. It essentially made the score Dad: 1,000; Mom: 1.

CHAPTER 27

Prince Of Shame:
An Unwinnable Paradox

Rock bottom became the solid foundation on which I built my life.

J.K. Rowling

It is a shameful, moral paradox knowing the mistakes you've made, the selfish wrong you've done, and knowing deep inside that if given the chance to do it all over again, it might well turn out the same.

But what of lessons learned?

It took thirty years for me to understand the always-festering relationship that had developed over the decades between my dad and me. I had the realization as I recalled that defining moment between him and his father, when my dad, a young farmer, wanted to show off some new farm equipment he'd acquired. All Dad wanted was a little praise. What he got was an insult from a man insecure in his own ways.

Insecurity, it seems, is our deplorable legacy.

We were like forcing the polar ends of a magnet toward one another. No matter how you positioned things, it just didn't work. But for as long as I rejected my father's behavior, and shunned his very presence, there was never a moment when I stopped trying to make him proud. There is no rest for a man who spends all his energy both resenting his father and chasing his approval. It's like chasing a ghost in a vacuum.

Rare is the father who wishes to hurt his son. And there's not a son anywhere whose natural instincts extend beyond making his dad proud. But it is a tricky relationship, this one between fathers and sons. One in which if passions run high enough, it gets off track quickly. And the longer it goes unrepaired, the more difficult it becomes getting it back in sync.

Generally, men shouldn't be allowed to make important decision before they're fifty. Our judgment is no better than children up until about forty. We spend the next ten years hiding our fragility, wondering what's wrong with us. But a few grains of wisdom assemble around fifty, if we're lucky.

At eighteen years old, I decided my father would never tell me what to do again. Ever. There is a sad, infinite lack of wisdom in that notion, but eighteen-year-old men think they know everything. Every time he alluded to my shortcomings, I reinforced it all the more. And saddest part of all, at its core it was more payback than self-protection. I spent nearly four decades punishing my father for his own misdeeds, all the while playing the role of some reputable community man. Under the veil, I was a coward and a hypocrite.

Rebellion is the surest sign of a man who is desperately lost. For years, I compensated for loss I never even knew was there. Never was there a sadder day than the one when I drove a new Mercedes off the show room floor, then pulled into the parking lot of an exclusive jewelry dealer and walked away with a Rolex. *I'll show him.* I never said it out loud, but it was always in my heart. *And he'll know that I did it without anything from him.*

In many ways, the retribution I so wrongly inflicted on Dad created the overachiever in me — not someone who was particularly great at lots of things, but rather someone who surpassed the little bit of natural talent he had through so many misguided feelings.

Three marathons completed. Paychecks amounting to more than I could spend. The power that came with politics during a six-year career on Capitol Hill. Projects on other continents. Walking across countries. Seven years since his passing, I look in the mirror and still see a little boy trying to make his father proud.

A handful of times my father told me he loved me.

Never once, did he say he was proud.

That ghost may never be caught.

CHAPTER 28

Biscuits & Gravy

I am free, no matter what rules surround me. If I find them tolerable, I tolerate them; if I find them too obnoxious, I break them. I am free because I know that I alone am morally responsible for everything I do.

Robert Heinlein

It wasn't a soulful love for the land, some proud aristocratic family lineage, or even a good income that drew my father to farming. It was, rather, chasing the thing he wanted most in his life. No rules.

But the funny thing about a person who runs from the rules of his own life, is just how strongly he will mandate a controlling set of rules over others. This is the one-way street rule breakers travel in so many of their relationships. Rule breakers by their nature, are occasional bullies.

For Watkins men, it is both the thing we most pursue, and our arch enemy. Freedom unchecked will drag a man through hell.

The American farmer is one of our land's few remaining frontiersmen. It's a livelihood where the possibilities are wide open and the outcome often a gamble, but the lifestyle is unmatched because there are no rules. No one tells you to get up at four o'clock in the morning. Nor do they tell you to watch the weather so you can run a cotton picker all night. And no one compels you to fair dealing with your neighbors or giving back to your community. The head of every farm family decides how he or she approaches all those things. It makes us, and it breaks us.

He could have easily been called the King of Secrets. Many were harmless, but some were devastating. The freedom that farming afforded my father oftentimes allowed him to break the rules of marital trust in ways frequently enough there was really never any recovery.

It wasn't enough to learn about the occasional missing twenty-five-hundred-dollar fuel bill, or a side loan at the bank somehow unrevealed. Our family home was mortgaged three times, twice without Mom's knowledge. And local bankers are always more than happy to play the no-lose game of loaning money to small farmers who hold land that increases in value every year. Mom was constantly digging her way out of a hole. Dad was always standing above, shoveling more debt on top of her.

The relief that came with my father's 1996 retirement was short-lived when this happened one last and devastating time. With no reason to believe any debt remained, Mom's daily trips to the

mailbox became a horror story that played out over the next six
months.

Over the years, Dad took a "rollover" option on a number of
loans, secretly pushing the due dates further and further out. One
day, a bill for eleven thousand dollars would appear. Eighteen
thousand the next. It amounted to an enormous sum that wiped
out their savings, and required them to mortgage crops of rental
income from the farm several years ahead. Retirement was never
as they had planned.

But at least he had his freedom, and no list of rules to obey.

There was a phrase Dad used through most of my childhood. It
was apparently his guiding philosophy for shaping my behavior.
In the early years, it was confusing. In the latter years, it just made
me angry.

"Do as I say, not as I do," he must have said it a thousand excruciating times.

For a young child, a statement like this is a deep paradox. *If he
can tell me the right thing, why doesn't he do it himself?* For an adolescent coming into a greater but fragile understanding about life,
it is a trigger. *Why should I obey the rules of someone who know-
ingly breaks them?*

It all reinforced a deep rebellion in my own life for forty years.
It's never been easy fitting into any place where there's always
someone telling you what to do. Structure is prison-like. Performance evaluations, a pain.

There will be one of two outcomes that arise between the shift-
ing plates of rebellion and freedom. Either you'll spend a lifetime

that's inauthentic and void of deeper meaning, or you'll realize there's something greater that's calling you to a different kind of opportunity.

By January 2012, all the years of smoking caught up with Daddy. And surrendering to a sedentary life inside his shop didn't help. The words had not yet been spoken, but the physicians' bedside manners said enough. My dad was dying. It wasn't easy seeing the man who broke all the rules and relished his freedom so much pushing an IV cart to the bathroom wearing a gown and being confined to a hospital bed. It was the picture of a man in surrendered misery. His defeat played out in a musty ten by ten hospital room with a bed pan at his side.

The combination of his medications and the natural effects of cardiopulmonary disorder caused all kinds of restrictions to Dad's diet. He never got anything much richer than a bowl of rice pudding or a cup of warm Jell-O.

One Sunday morning it was just Mom, Dad, and me in the room and we were discussing old times like the occasional Sunday breakfast we'd share sitting together at our kitchen bar.

"I tell you, these people are starving me here. I can't remember when I've had any good food," he said.

Suddenly, something came over the rule breaker in me. *Here's a man who's dying, he wants some good food and they're bringing him Jell-O.*

"I'll be right back." I said.

The hospital's cafeteria was known for its above-average food, and I recalled an unusually good breakfast from years earlier when each of my children was born there. Walking off the elevator toward the service area, I saw exactly what I'd come for.

"Give me two biscuits with extra gravy and two pieces of sausage, please," I asked the lady behind the counter. I paid, and in moments was headed back toward the room. It couldn't have made me any happier handing him a tray full of gold.

"What's this?" he looked at the heavy Styrofoam container.

"Open it up and take a look," I grinned.

Smiling wide, he looked at me and Mom, almost as if asking permission to go against everything the medical staff had instructed. It's a look to which we were both unaccustomed.

"It's up to you, but I do believe I'd eat every crumb of it," I said. "Might just cure you altogether."

Watching Dad for the next five minutes is one of my life's best memories. If the plastic utensils had been metal, the sparks would have started a fire in the room's pure oxygen atmosphere.

As he finished, he leaned back, exhaled and closed his eyes in a way that expressed a certain look of satisfaction I'd rarely seen on the man's face.

"Best I ever had," and he trailed off into a nap.

It was the best moment we'd ever shared, breaking the rules together as a team of rebels.

CHAPTER 29

Nothing To Forgive

Closure is when raw memory blurs to become the folklore of life.

Steward Stafford

What exactly *is* a normal family?

Best-selling South Carolina author Pat Conroy became famous for the vivid, often troubling, picture he painted of his own family life. A military-style tyrant of a physically abusive father, a controlling and manipulative mother, and chronically depressed, schizophrenic, and suicidal siblings. With Conroy's storytelling, everything was on the table.

More than once, interviewers asked Conroy if he believed in normal families. On those occasions, he often did what he did best. He told a story.

He was the featured draw at an Atlanta book signing where what he described as "the most beautiful couple you could imagine" approached the signing table. "I'm guessing he was president of his fraternity, and she was the president of her sorority at the University of Georgia," he said. "They were the most perfect people you've ever laid eyes on."

He signed their books, engaged in the normal chit chat, and the couple walked away together hand in hand. It was just a few seconds before the handsome man turned with an afterthought he couldn't keep to himself. Conroy heard it frequently.

"Your family was crazy weren't they?" he asked from a distance.

Conroy paused, smiled, and thought about a reply.

"Sure were," another pause as he weighed his words. "How's your family?"

"Oh, they're all great. We've never been better."

"Well hey, let me ask you something, pal," Conroy began. "And I want you to think about this. How far back do you have to go in your family before you hit crazy? Think about it. Mom? Dad? A brother? Uncle?"

"They're all great. Not a crazy one in the bunch," the man said.

His wife could stand it no longer before she interjected dramatically.

"His mother's a lunatic! She should be in an insane asylum!"

Think about it.

How far back must you go in your family to find the one who loves life so much they screw it up a lot with some very bad decisions? Who is the insecure relative compensating at every turn? Who is the one standing in the circle, hand outstretched, just waiting for a friend?

How far back must you go to find the David Watkins in your family?

In rural America in the 1980s, we lived in the fantasy that every family outside ours was normal. All the while my father was drunk and demanding that I lie for him, I envisioned all the other families along Highbanks Road sitting down to the perfect dinner, contemplating their day, and planning the next family vacation. In reality, those families were dealing with their own personal challenges — drug problems, financial worries, even incest in a home no farther from ours than you could shoot a sling shot.

What you realize across time is that no one sets out to hurt other people. Everyone's a product of that from which they come, and most of us work to be better from one generation to the next. Because we're human, we have our setbacks.

As a storyteller, I keep notes everywhere. There's a notebook in the truck console, not to mention a handheld recorder. Another notebook sits beside my favorite relaxing chair, and yet another bedside. There's one specifically for inspiration that comes at church. And a smartphone app covers everything in between. My least favorite time of the month is the day I gather all the notes, scatter them across the kitchen table, and organize them in a big three-ring binder I use as a master notebook. It's the place where all my story ideas go until it's time to place them in a more formal text. That book goes everywhere with me, and it's a practice I've kept for years.

Several years ago that monthly exercise brought an amazing revelation.

As I flipped through the hundreds of pages, scribbled hand-written notes and orange highlighted lines all about, some on coffee-stained pages, a common denominator became obvious.

So many of the stories I'd recalled from childhood and ado-lescence were the product of a life richer than most. There was nothing hum-drum about where I'd come from, or the way my young life was shaped. Dad had carried me along to experience the thrill of mallard ducks sailing into a river pond. He'd exposed me to other men who shared stories of war and their youth during the Great Depression. He'd shown me, through his own actions, what it was like to struggle against the elements and make a living on a small farm. He did none of it perfectly, but he took me along for a ride where every experience shaped me. Mom was the love, consistency, and stability for everything in between.

It was incredible, really, how much time I'd wasted resenting it all. And all that while, there was nothing to forgive. If anything, so much of it was a gift more valuable than money can buy.

Thank goodness I got the chance to tell him that.

And what an amazing experience it's been learning to love home again.

CHAPTER 30

The Reckless Pursuit Of Grace

Thou hast formed us for Thyself, and our hearts are restless till they find rest in Thee.

St. Augustine

We will never stop trying to figure out God's ways. And He will never stop loving us for trying.

But the fact is, the God of the universe, Creator of all things, Sovereign of all that has been, is, and will be, operates in ways that we'll never understand. He works for a purpose that transcends our thinking, and nothing about Him fits in a box.

If God is anything, He is *beyond*.

Our efforts to understand Him feel like we're running on a treadmill. The exercise is great, but in the end, we're still pretty much right where we started.

Or are we?

Watching someone die is one of the most surreal experiences a person can know. As you witness those final moments when a friend or relative slips from this world to the next, it's almost as if you participate in their transition to eternity. The final breaths of the living are sometimes a struggle. The body wants to stay. The soul longs for home.

As a participant in this process, I've temporarily set aside inevitable grief, and encouraged loved ones with assurances that it's okay to go home. We pray the suffering will subside quickly and that peace shepherds our loved ones into the discovery of a glorious realm.

We wish there were so much more we could do. But all God really allows in these moments is our presence. Just on the other side, so close and yet so far, eternity's will is fulfilled.

So simple in its nature. So overwhelming to understand.

For those who live a life into their seventies or eighties, many will eventually make an important subconscious decision. Somewhere inside themselves, they will one day decide to continue living abundantly, or they will succumb to circumstances, and begin the slow, often painful process of dying. It's the essence of a notable line offered from the thoughtful movie character "Red" Redding at the sudden reality of his forty years in Shawshank prison.

Get busy living, or get busy dying.

When my dad finally moved from our countryside farm to urban Jonesboro, Arkansas, I watched helplessly as he decided to stop living. It was seven precious years before his actual death that he decided he'd spend his remaining days in a tool shed, lying on a couch watching television, and playing the occasional round of online poker. The man who was once the king of good times surrendered almost all for which he'd been known.

Though the last twenty years of his life were smoke free, my dad never lost the craving for a cigarette. It was habit. He smoked when he drank, when he was happy, when he was angry or upset. He just didn't give it up soon enough.

He lived his last several years coping with chronic obstructive pulmonary disease. It's a horrible death sentence that robs its victims of mobility and just about every enjoyable activity. Carrying an oxygen tank and a mask around everywhere is no way to live.

Just as it is with raising children, something instinctively parent-like kicks in when it comes to our own parents' well-being. In the volatile relationship with my father, I found the instinct went beyond concerns of physical care. It was almost like a complete parent-child role reversal.

Until his last weeks, there weren't more than one or two times when Dad and I had a serious conversation about God. Even though there was little fruit to show for it, I felt as though he believed in God, but never understood the good parts of the simple gospel and the immediate freedom of forgiveness that comes by faith through grace. The more resigned he grew to an unforgiven soul, the more urgent it became for me to help free him of those bonds. It was selfish in many ways. I couldn't imagine eternity separated from my father. And it was a heavy responsibility in other ways. Among all his relationships, I couldn't imagine anyone else who would take the initiative to help him. The greater the burden grew, the more barriers there seemed to surmount.

Why the most important things in life are usually the most difficult is a mystery. The course of my disobedience to this calling over the next several years was exhausting, but never more so than the afternoon the barrier came down in that tool shed where we spent five hours talking, praying, crying, and me leaving with a sense that we'd checked all the boxes. Two weeks later, we got into an argument and didn't speak for six months. I wasn't sure either of us had changed.

Sometimes, you think you're done dealing with the past, but the past isn't finished with you.

As his respiratory illness worsened, Dad spent the last six months of his life in and out of the hospital. He simply couldn't get enough oxygen into his body to function. In January 2012, we read between the lines of several doctors' delicate bedside manners. Dad would never go home.

The reality of a date with death brings out the best in families. Mom, exhausted as Dad's primary caretaker, became clear-eyed, decisive, and laser focused on his comfort. Extended family gathered in the hospital room regularly laughing and sharing stories. Even I took on the role of compassionate son as if the decades of my indifference suddenly mattered not, but knowing better.

As for Dad, fully aware where all this was going, something inside him was changing. It was authentic and undeniable. Sometimes God gives us this precious opportunity to say goodbye. It's bittersweet because it is goodbye, but at least you get to say it. One afternoon he called me to the bedside, held my hand, and placed his other hand on my face. Mom sat in a corner chair pretending not to be there.

"I'm sorry, Son," his blue eyes peered into mine. It was the most sincere thing I'd ever heard him speak.

"I'm sorry, too, Dad," I choked out, burying my watering eyes into his chest. It's the only time I remember ever feeling completely secure in his embrace. I could have stayed there forever.

"I know you will, but I need you to take care of your mama. She's going to need you."

"I will."

The next seven days leading to his death are a time to which I've often attempted to assign some words. Nothing, even now, seems adequate to describe that refining week. It's one of those scenarios where you so desperately wish you could understand the way God works. Ultimately, I am resigned to the idea that perhaps all things are not for knowing this side of Heaven.

Dad had spent enough Easter evenings watching television as Charlton Heston carried tablets down from a mountain that Dad believed those rules, carved in stone, dictated his destiny. Until the end, he never quite grasped how the gospel means the end of scorekeeping — that we are no longer defined by our best or our worst moment. We believe God comes in, wipes the slate clean, and we get a new beginning. He actually takes the slate, breaks it across His knee, and says, "You are no longer defined by your performance. The contest is won."

But in that last week, everything changed. You could feel it with every sense. There was a new tenderness in Daddy's touch, a deeper light in his ice-blue eyes, and a soothing tone to his once harsh voice. In what easily could have been the most uncertain moments of his life, he made *us* all feel better.

I am yet to understand what happened those last few days in that hospital room. Maybe it was divine revelation, some epiphany, or perhaps a holy experience. Maybe some distant realm an angel defeated the demon that haunted my dad a lifetime. But God spoke to my dad. Eternity altered at the hand of the Lord, angels rejoiced. And so did I.

Six days later and less than twenty-four hours after entering hospice, he took his last shallow breath on Earth. Mercy covered justice as he exhaled his last.

All the while I'd been working so hard to fast-forward my father into some academic grace, God was doing the real work, in slow motion, one small step at a time, and encouraging him with a gentle whisper. He is beyond.

First Kings 19 recounts the story of God's faithful prophet Elijah, who fleeing the rebellious Israelites for fear of his life, found himself one day inside a cave. It was there that God showed him something that seems contrary to all we believe we know about the Creator of the Universe:

> *The Lord said, "Go out and stand on the mountain in the presence of the Lord, for the Lord is about to pass by." Then a great and powerful wind tore the mountains apart and shattered the rocks before the Lord, but the Lord was not in the wind. After the wind there was an earthquake, but the Lord was not in the earthquake. After the earthquake came a fire, but the Lord was not in the fire. And after the fire came a gentle whisper.*
>
> *1 Kings 19:11-12*

And so it was with my father. The man who looked for life's greatest pleasure in all the big things found his eternity in a still, small voice.

Every year, dads across America buy their young sons one of those cheap, plastic, toy lawn mowers. They resemble the push-type mower, and are often the highlight of spring Easter basket gift collections. Have you ever seen a young father out mowing the yard, his four-year-old son not far behind with his own plastic machine? Nothing thrills a young boy more. He believes he's really lending a helping hand.

So it is with our Kingdom work here on earth, especially when it comes to sharing the gospel's good news with family and friends. God is just like the dad mowing the yard. He doesn't need the son's help, for he's quite capable all on his own. But he graciously and generously allows us to play a role in His greater economy. And what may seem like a burden as we're experiencing it is, in fact, an unsurpassed joy in retrospect. We simply can't know His design for how it will all play out. There is no standard measure.

In both the Greek and the Hebrew are words interchangeable with the definition of wind, breath, and spirit. The Hebrew *ruach*, and the Greek *pneuma*. Though he did not come to Elijah in the wind, God is as the wind, blowing wherever he wishes, sometimes seen or even heard, but surpassing our knowledge of where He comes from or where He is going.

If the outcome is the same, does it even matter *when* a person comes to faith, as long as they *do come*?

If a man like my father can experience divine revelation that gives him the same benefit package as someone who's served the Kingdom faithfully for seventy years, does any of this, aside from the risk of knowing when we'll die, differentiate anything? Did he miss something other people find? If everything's perfect in Heaven, how does our life's timeline matter here on Earth?

Are fruits of the spirit equal just as long as there's something in the bowl?

Of course our time on Earth matters, else the omniscient God would never have us here in the first place. It may be one of the most misconstrued notions of the faith. The Christ follower's goal isn't the afterlife. It's using the time we have here to grow *more like Christ*. It's the adventure of pursuing Him:

> *Therefore, be imitators of God, as beloved children; and walk in love, just as Christ also loved you and gave Himself up for us, an offering and a sacrifice to God as a fragrant aroma.*
>
> *Ephesians 5:1-2*

As we grow in Christ fulfilling the commandments to serve the poor, heal the brokenhearted, and love our neighbors as we love ourselves, we are storing future heavenly rewards for a life in eternity, often wrongly portrayed as lying around on a cloud, strumming a harp, bored to tears. The Bible makes it clear that we will all have responsibilities in Heaven, and on the New Earth, and those responsibilities will vary according to the fruits of our labor on earth:

Do not store up for yourselves treasures on earth, where moths and vermin destroy, and where thieves break in and steal. But store up for yourselves treasures in heaven...
                                              Matthew 6:19-20

So neither the one who plants nor the one who waters is anything, but only God, who makes things grow. The one who plants and the one who waters have one purpose, and they will each be rewarded according to their own labor.
                                              1 Corinthians 3:7-8

Brethren, I do not regard myself as having laid hold of it yet; but one thing I do: forgetting what lies behind and reaching forward to what lies ahead, I press on toward the goal for the prize of the upward call of God in Christ Jesus.
                                              Philippians 3:13-14

Yes. Life on earth matters, and time is precious.

Dad's life on earth probably didn't give him rule of a heavenly nation, and I doubt he's involved in creating new dimensions across the universe.

But I bet he's a great caretaker for an awesome forty-acre patch of cotton in some picturesque land where he produces six bales per acre, and the cotton is spun into gold.

CHAPTER 31

Perfect Peace: Behold The Proof

Joy is not produced because others praise you. Joy emanates unbidden and unforced. Joy comes as a gift when you least expect it. At those fleeting moments you know why you were put here and what truth you serve. You may not feel giddy at those moments, you may not hear the orchestra's delirious swell or see flashes of crimson and gold, but you will feel a satisfaction, a silence, a peace—a hush. Those moments are the blessings and the signs of a beautiful life.

David Brooks
The Road to Character

I've never been good at sitting still for long. Even when the writing flows well, after just a few hundred words it's necessary to walk around a bit. Moving is as much a part of my creative process as thinking or drinking coffee. Long, drawn-out formal dinners lasting for hours are agony. Just a quick walk out the back door, and a look at the garden creates a nice reset.

It was just as true a few years ago when I accepted a short-term job helping people find jobs through a local Goodwill Store. Most store employees grew accustomed to my casual walk up and down the aisles every hour. But one morning, a customer I'd never seen walked up from behind and offered a random thought that caused me to think about my growing relationship with Jesus the rest of that day and beyond.

"Mister, you look and walk as though you don't have a care in the world."

Just a little surprised, I fumbled for a polite response.

"Well, now that you mention it, I don't believe I do."

But perfect peace was not something that came naturally to me, or my father.

In 2008, my world crumbled.

After nearly twenty years of marriage, I now carried the stigma of a divorced man. Then, something they called the Great Recession came along and wiped out a several-hundred-thousand-dollar investment I'd put into building a new career. I was broke. Relationships with some of the people I loved the very most, including my father and my own children, were in shambles. The anxiety and the dread of each day became so bad that I woke up in full-blown convulsions every morning for nearly a year. And for the first moment in my life, tomorrow was unknown. You will never find peace in a man who is completely and desperately lost. Depression robs you of the best of your identity. It tells you lies about the rest.

But this was more than a situation of external circumstances. Something had stirred a rebellion inside me. Looking back, I can see the pride, the lack of concern for others, and the downright hypocrisy in a life where I lived the public role of a good and decent man. God never lets you get by with these things. He does not take kindly to our mocking. In my case, it was a kind of false role playing on his behalf. Thank goodness that He brings discipline to those he loves. It's easier to say that now. At the time, not so much.

The three years that followed brought the most intensely painful experiences I'd known, so much that I still prefer not ruminating on them for long. God's grace, and my wife's and mom's unconditional love and presence, facilitated a path to the other side of a dark abyss. In the summer of 2015, I decided to celebrate the beginning of that healing, and listen for what might come next in life.

So I went on a long walk.

El Camino de Santiago, translated The Way of St. James, is one of the most ancient Christian pilgrimages in the world. It begins in any one of dozens of locations across Europe, and concludes in Santiago de Compostela, where it is believed the remains of St. James, apostle of Jesus, are enshrined in a sarcophagus beneath a centuries-old cathedral. I'd read about the pilgrimage, even seen a movie and a documentary about it. A long walk in a place I'd never been along the hallowed grounds of an apostle and his work spoke to my spirit. That October, I took the first steps of a five-hundred-mile walk across Spain's Iberian Peninsula. There were no tour groups. No sight-seeing guides. Just me.

Walking fifteen miles a day for forty days with nothing but a pair of shoes and backpack to your name creates a minimalist kind of lifestyle that alters your senses. Food tastes better. Birds chirping inside the dense country fencerows sound sweeter. The sky is bigger, bluer, more expansive in a way that can't help but make you think about some kind of divine creation. On pilgrimage, I found less noise and more clarity, which was exactly what I needed, even if God didn't show up and blind me along some Damascus Road.

After five days of walking, I felt something I'd not known for a long time. I'd crossed a challenging mountain range, walked four hours through a cloud storm, been lost three or four times, and had walked more than fifty miles. For the first time on day five, I stopped for a moment, turned around and looked back, where I could see the distance I'd come. It was astonishing. It was a moment that brought not only peace, but the most pristine clarity I'd had about life in nearly four years. And it was so unexpectedly simple. From the next step forward and beyond, I promised myself I'd never live life as a hypocrite again. I would pursue the truth, meditate on the truth, and do my best to exemplify the truth. That's all that mattered now.

Knowing just a little about Jesus may well be more detrimental than knowing nothing at all. There was a time in my own life — and I've seen it in others including Dad — where it was safe to say we knew just enough about Jesus to be dangerous.

Almost inevitably that shallow depth of superficial knowledge will lead to self-condemnation, a lack of self-worth, and a life standard that's impossible to live. It was exactly what my father experienced. All he could see was a legalistic, lawful view that God himself knew, which condemned us all. But as we keep walking with God, asking forgiveness for our hypocrisy, and setting out on a genuine pursuit of the truth, we'll discover the grace that sets us free.

For so many painful years, Dad was so consumed with the idea of such an angry God that he had a hard time seeing the God who loved him. Feeling completely unworthy, he'd given up more than once. But as long as there is a spark of desire or a mustard seed of hope, God draws us all toward Him. Ultimately, whatever it is we decide to do with His drawing power, He leaves that choice to us.

CHAPTER 32

Fathers, Sons, & The Father

*Learn to love people for who they are, and forgive them for
who they are not.*

Tim Russert

The 1998 mid-term election was three months past and we were
all just beginning to find our stride as a sixteen-member congres-
sional staff that answered to a quarter of a million constituents.
All of us, including the candidate, had met the challenge of a high
learning curve, the equivalent of which was getting thrown off the
pier and into the deep water. Washington politics is sink or swim,
and you'd better find your rhythm fast.

It was a Saturday afternoon. Fall in the Ozark foothills, air as
fresh as morning dew. The winding highway pig-trailed through
the forests painted in rich reds, greens, and golds. As we drove
toward the next community event where they literally had street

races with outhouses on wheels, I took advantage of the peaceful moment to ask my new boss how it felt serving as a new member of the United States Congress. He studied a moment. His answer was unexpected to the both of us, I think, signaled by the uncommon break in his steady voice.

"What I keep thinking about is election night and how much I wish my dad had been there," the congressman said. "He would have never imagined anything like this, but I want to think he would've been proud."

One of five hundred thirty-five of the most elite and powerful people in the world, still trying to make his father proud.

It is arguably the most difficult relationship on the planet, this connection between father and son. Maybe it is the father's innate drive to teach the son to become a man. Or maybe it is just as naturally the son's instinct to rebel and become his own man. Perhaps it's as simple as waning testosterone versus exploding testosterone. But there is an undeniable volatility.

Masculinity is not a bad thing. If anything, we need more of it in a world that wants to make its men, well, more feminine. God knew what He was doing in the creation of male and female. But there can be too much of a good thing. There is nothing good about a masculinity that grows toxic. Across time, a boy's relationship with his father will shape a lot about how he lives life as a man. And it may be the difficult maneuvering of this relationship that creates so many barriers to a deeper knowledge of God. It's not so easy comprehending the unconditional love of a Father you can't see, when the one right in front of you is cussing up a blue streak and you're wondering if he's about to punch you in the face. This is one of our great disconnects — the imperfection of the earthly father versus the perfect love of God the Father almighty.

In retrospect, it was the disconnect with my own dad that ultimately compelled a greater knowledge of the heavenly Father. It seemed for years, I'd been told what I believed. There came a time when it was important to determine for myself exactly what I believed and why.

What I discovered was a divine creator who always had my best interest at heart, even if there were times when I didn't feel so loved. I found:

- Loving correction;
- Provision for my needs;
- Wisdom, and most importantly,
- A never-ending welcome back.

In the story of the prodigal son, a wayward and rebellious boy, most likely frustrated with his father's corrective oversight, takes his inheritance and leaves home. He wishes to go his own way and cast all the rules aside. And it's true, for a time he lives the high life, prominent on the social scene, probably impressing all the young girls. Then one day all the unchecked freedom catches up with him. He's broke, without friends, no better than the pigs whose muddy sty he now shares as a bed. He now longs for home, but fears his father's wrath. Maybe even more troubling are the son's feelings about his own unworthiness.

What happens?

And he arose and came to his father. But while he was still a long way off, his father saw him and felt compassion, and ran and embraced him and kissed him.

Luke 15: 20

The vision of the father *running* toward his wayward son is one that never gets old.

Whose behavior here was more lavish? The son's partying, but temporary lifestyle? Or, the father's grand celebration that his son had returned home?

The parable, sometimes known as "The Lovesick Father," makes it clear.

We are always welcome home.

Journalist Vance Fry wrote that throughout the gospels, Jesus makes more than one hundred fifty references to God as a father. For the Jews of that time, this was a new way of addressing God. While Old Testament writers sometimes described God using qualities of earthly fathers (and mothers), Jesus referred to God using more informal, intimate language such as Abba Father, perhaps best translated as "daddy." He also invites us into this relationship, teaching us to address God as "our Father in heaven." It's only through Christ's work on the cross that we are adopted into this family relationship.

It is fortunate for my dad there are no real rules in this simple equation. The Father, indeed, adopts us, redeems us, and asks only one thing of us — and it's not so much, in light of the evidence.

He asks that we believe.

As we make that choice, we unlock the currency of The Kingdom, and there is no limit to the expense account our Father will direct toward us.

AFTERWORD

*We leave, we run away and don't realize how much we'll
need to go back home one day. The South is like that. It's
the worst mama in the world, and it's the best mama in
the world.*

James McBride

I live in the city now, but still get a little nostalgic looking at the
criss-crossed jet contrails as they fade in the western sky around
sunset. It evokes the same feelings of wonderment and an appetite for adventure I had all those years ago as a boy who lived in
the middle of nowhere.

What a relief it is now not to look back on that place as I once
did. Hate is so exhausting. Not only did I see my father find his
perfect peace. In the process, I have learned to love home again.

Someone asked recently, "How can you write an entire book
about an old dirt road?"

It occurred to me, because of the question, just how much of
my life was shaped on that very place. It's true, this is a book much

about two men — one young, one older — learning how to maneuver the tricky life and their relationship on a cotton farm during the 1980s. It is just as much a tribute to a rural way of life we'll never again know.

Any project like this is easy to romanticize. Time has a way of sifting the bad memories from the good. I've tried to avoid those romantic feelings and keep the wrecking ball in perspective. It was a tough life on that cotton farm. A thousand variables could destroy your best efforts, and sometimes they did. But it was a rich life. A place where we learned about disappointment and joy, redemption and reconciliation. It was a place where, every year, we watched with our own eyes as God made all things new. We prayed for sunshine and rain, and told Him we'd do the rest.

Many of the people you read about in this book are depicted by name, and portrayed just as they are. Many who had an impact on my family's life are not included. The colorful and the crazy are always the easiest to write about, but I am grateful for an abundance of good Arkansas folk who did their due diligence every day and had some part in my raising. I love them, every one.

Many a night throughout the writing this book, I dreamed of my dad. One night, he walked through a door in a picture so vivid I could almost touch him. In the all the months of writing, there wasn't a single bad dream.

I once considered it a stigma to come from a dysfunctional family. I've since learned there's no such thing as normal. We didn't live a boring life. Not even close.

And I thank God for it, and how it created some of the richest stories a person can tell.

-THE END-

ABOUT THE AUTHOR

Steve Watkins is an award-winning author who writes to encourage readers about pursuing intentional quests and taking responsibility for a deeper knowledge of who they are. His first book, Pilgrim Strong: Rewriting My Story on the Way of St. James, recounted the inner journey of his 500-mile pilgrimage across Spain. He and his wife, Dana live in the Ozark Mountains of Arkansas where he is the founder of the Tranquility Base Retreat Center for Writers and Thinkers, and is a staff writer for the Stone County Leader. He loves chicken and dressing, barbecue, and sweet iced tea.

Visit his website at

STEVE-WATKINS.COM

Made in the USA
Monee, IL
01 October 2020